KB263440

Dr. Kim's
KOREAN
for Complete Beginners

YOUNG G. KIM

(주)박이정

To Danny and David,
who were my first students

Preface

This book is your guide on a great adventure. Learning Korean is the key to understanding Korean and Korea, from traditional folk tales all the way up to today's dynamic worlds of popular culture and technological innovation. Together we will begin this journey by exploring and using the unfamiliar sounds, symbols, and rules that compose this language.

At the heart of this textbook is my belief that learning a new language is achieved not only through the study of its linguistic elements, but also by means of a thorough grasp of the culture it expresses. Just as we learn sounds, vocabulary, and grammar, we'll also learn about Korean culture, thought, and history. In this respect, learning a new language is an integrative effort involving intellectual and cultural engagement.

In my four decades of teaching Korean, my focus has always been on how to explain linguistic structures and principles in the clearest and simplest way possible. Similarly, in creating this text, I have tried to make all concepts and content easy to understand and easy to acquire. While I keep complex linguistic explanations and theory to a minimum, I break down important concepts and present them using practical terms and simple structures.

Of course, this book is also a reflection of my experiences in the classroom. I share the pleasure of publishing this text with my former students at the University of Toronto and the University of Waterloo who learned how to read, write, and speak Korean with great enthusiasm and dedication. I would also like to express my gratitude to the teaching assistants and students who have offered valuable comments and practical suggestions, as well as to the colleagues who have provided collegiality and support over the years.

Now let's begin our journey to master the Korean language!

Young G. Kim

Toronto, Canada

Contents

Contents

Introduction

The Korean Language and Korean Writing System

With nearly 80 million native speakers in the Korean peninsula and around the world, the Korean language is one of the world's most spoken languages. It belongs to the Altaic languages, which is comprised of languages like Turkish, Mongolian, Manchurian, and Tungusic.

Throughout its history, Korea has been geographically surrounded by China, Russia and Japan. As such, it has a long and complicated political and cultural relationship with these surrounding countries, particularly China and Japan.

Many non-Korean speakers assume that the Korean Language might be similar to Chinese and Japanese. The Korean and Japanese languages are similar in terms of grammatical structure, but the pronunciation and vocabulary bases are quite different.

On the other hand, Korean and Chinese are completely different languages. Koreans used Chinese characters in their literary life until the Korean writing system was invented. The use of Chinese characters have had a considerable impact on Korean vocabulary. A great deal of Korean vocabulary is derived from Chinese characters. Altogether, the impact of Chinese characters on Korean and other East Asian languages is similar to impact that Latin has had on many European languages.

The Korean writing system called 'Hangeul' was developed by a group of scholars in 15th century, which was directed by King Sejong of the Chosun Dynasty. In contrast to Chinese characters, which have ideographic and pictographic features, Korean characters are phonetic scripts like the letters of the English alphabet. Because the Korean writing system is scientifically derived and systematically organized, it is possible for someone to learn the writing system easily in as little as a few days or even hours.

The Steps to Learn the Writing System

'Hangeul,' the writing system of the Korean language, is a phonetic script where a character corresponds to a particular sound. Thus, learning all the necessary sounds of Korean and its corresponding characters simultaneously isthe most effective way of learning the Korean writing system. In this way, learning the Korean writing system takes only a matter of hours for a beginner. The following are the steps to learning the sounds of Korean vowels and consonants and their corresponding characters:

Step 1:

Listen a few times to the pronunciation of a sound produced by a Korean teacher or a native speaker, and then imitate the sound until you can pronounce it accurately. I strongly advise you repeat this practice to obtain satisfactory results with sufficient time and patience, just like babies imitate the sounds of their mothers. Language is made up of sounds, so if one does not acquire the ability to listen to necessary sounds as well as the ability to pronounce all necessary sounds, then naturally, one cannot acquire the ability to use the language for communication.

Step 2:

Continuously practice writing the corresponding character in the right order of strokes until you have it memorized. Practice how to write each character looking at the writing order of vowels and consonants chart, found on page 11. After you learn one sound and one character, move on to the next one. Then, repeat these steps until you have finished all of the sounds of the Korean vowels and consonants and their corresponding characters.

If you are in a situation where it is not possible to get practical help from a teacher or a native speaker, you could also practice your pronunciation using the recordings of demonstrated pronunciations. In case you have to practice only based on written explanation and instruction, I strongly suggest you confirm with a teacher or a native speaker that your pronunciation is natural and acceptable.

Korean Vowels and Consonants

The following explanation regarding the actual pronunciation of Korean vowels and consonants is presented for the convenience of students who understand English. There are a few systems that transcribe Korean pronunciation into Romanization. In this text, one particular system has been adopted with a minor revision. However, one should not take these Romanized symbols as they understand the English alphabet. These Romanized symbols are used just for phonetic transcription of the sounds. Thus, throughout this book, the symbols appearing in square brackets are all phonetic transcriptions, not English spellings.

1. Vowels

The characters representing Korean vowels can be categorized into three types in terms of shapes.

Type 1: One or two long vertical lines or one or two short lines at the left or
       right of the vertical lines:

ㅣ, ㅏ, ㅑ, ㅓ, ㅕ, ㅐ, ㅒ, ㅔ, ㅖ

Type 2: A long horizontal line or one or two short lines either up or down from
       the horizontal line:

ㅡ, ㅗ, ㅛ, ㅜ, ㅠ

Type 3: Combinations of the above two types:

ㅘ, ㅝ, ㅚ, ㅟ, ㅙ, ㅞ, ㅢ

The above characters representing Korean vowels and their pronunciations will be presented one by one in the following six groups. The Korean characters are written with a certain order of strokes. The writing steps will be presented in a chart after the introduction of characters and pronunciation.

ㅏ	[a]	is pronounced like 'a' in 'father' or 'ah!'
ㅓ	[eo]	is pronounced like 'u' in 'under'
ㅗ	[o]	is pronounced like 'o' in 'owe'
ㅜ	[u]	is pronounced like 'oo' in 'pool'
ㅡ	[eu]	is pronounced like 'u' in 'put'
ㅣ	[i]	is pronounced like 'ee' in 'cheese'
ㅑ	[ya]	is pronounced like 'ya'in 'yard'
ㅕ	[yeo]	is pronounced like 'you' in 'young'
ㅛ	[yo]	is pronounced like 'yo' in 'yoyo'
ㅠ	[yu]	is pronounced like 'you' in 'you'
ㅔ	[e]	is pronounced like 'e' in 'egg' or 'e' in 'bet'
ㅐ	[ae]	is pronounced like 'a' in 'at' or 'a' in 'bank'
ㅖ	[ye]	is pronounced like 'ye' in 'yes'
ㅒ	[yae]	is pronounced like 'ya' in 'yank'
ㅘ	[wa]	is pronounced like 'wa' in 'watt'
ㅝ	[wo]	is pronounced like 'wo' in 'wonder'
ㅚ	[oe]	is pronounced like 'wa' in 'way'
ㅟ	[wi]	is pronounced like 'we' in 'we'
ㅙ	[wae]	is pronounced like 'wa' in 'wagon' or 'waiver'
ㅞ	[we]	is pronounced like 'we' in 'well' or 'Wendy'
ㅢ	[ui]	is pronounced like 'uoy' in 'buoy'

2. Consonants

The characters representing Korean consonants are derived from five basic forms:

1) ㄱ 〉 ㅋ 〉 ㄲ

2) ㄴ 〉 ㄷ 〉 ㅌ 〉 ㄹ 〉 ㄸ

3) ㅁ 〉 ㅂ 〉 ㅍ 〉 ㅃ

4) ㅅ 〉 ㅈ 〉 ㅊ 〉 ㅆ 〉 ㅉ

5) ㅇ 〉 ㅎ

However, the Korean consonants will be presented in the conventional way:

ㄱ [g, k] in the initial position of a syllable it is pronounced like 'g' in 'gun', when it appears at the end of a syllable it is pronounced as 'k' in 'slack'

ㄴ [n] is pronounced like 'n' in 'neat'

ㄷ [d / t] is pronounced like 'd' in 'dog'. When it appears at the end of a syllable it is pronounced as 't' in 'rot'

ㄹ [r / l] is pronounced like 'r' in 'radio' in the initial position of a syllable, or 'l' in 'until' in the final position of a syllable

ㅁ [m] is pronounced like 'm' in 'mother'

ㅂ [b, p] in the initial sound of a syllable it is pronounced like 'b' in 'boy', and in the final sound of a syllable it is pronounced as 'p' in 'pop'

ㅅ [s] is pronounced like 's' in 'spring'

ㅇ [ng] is pronounced like 'ng' in 'ping', or, it does not have any phonetic value in the initial position of a syllable

ㅈ [j] is pronounced like 'j' in 'Jenny'

ㅊ [ch] is pronounced like 'ch' in 'cheese'

ㅋ [k] is pronounced like 'k' in 'kid'

ㅌ [t] is pronounced like 't' in 'tee'

ㅍ [p] is pronounced like 'p' in 'ping'

ㅎ [h] is pronounced like 'h' in 'hen'

ㄲ [kk] is pronounced like 'k' in 'sky'

ㄸ [tt] is pronounced like 't' in 'stick'

ㅃ [pp] is pronounced like 'p' in 'spy'

ㅆ [ss] is pronounced like 's' in 'sink'

ㅉ [jj] is pronounced like 'ts' in 'cuts'

Writing Order of Vowels and Consonants

Korean characters are generally written from top to bottom, and they are written left to right. The table below shows how to write the characters in the proper order of strokes.

1) The Stroke Order of Characters: Vowels

Character	Name	1	2	3	4	5
ㅏ	아 [a]	ㅣ	ㅏ			
ㅓ	어 [eo]	-	ㅓ			
ㅗ	오 [o]	ㆍ	ㅗ			
ㅜ	우 [u]	—	ㅜ			
ㅡ	으 [eu]	—				
ㅣ	이 [i]	ㅣ				
ㅑ	야 [ya]	ㅣ	ㅏ	ㅑ		
ㅕ	여 [yeo]	-	ㅍ	ㅕ		
ㅛ	요 [yo]	ㆍ	ㅛ	ㅛ		
ㅠ	유 [yu]	—	ㅜ	ㅠ		
ㅔ	에 [e]	-	ㅓ	ㅔ		
ㅐ	애 [ae]	ㅣ	ㅏ	ㅐ		
ㅖ	예 [ye]	-	ㅍ	ㅕ	ㅖ	
ㅒ	얘 [yae]	ㅣ	ㅏ	ㅑ	ㅒ	
ㅘ	와 [wa]	ㆍ	ㅗ	ㅚ	ㅘ	
ㅝ	워 [wo]	—	ㅜ	ㅜ	ㅝ	
ㅚ	외 [oe]	ㆍ	ㅗ	ㅚ		
ㅟ	위 [wi]	—	ㅜ	ㅟ		
ㅙ	왜 [wae]	ㆍ	ㅗ	ㅚ	ㅘ	ㅙ
ㅞ	웨 [we]	—	ㅜ	ㅜ	ㅝ	ㅞ
ㅢ	의 [ui]	—	ㅢ			

2) The Stroke Order of Characters: Consonants

Character	Name	1	2	3	4
ㄱ	기역 [gi-yeok]	ㄱ			
ㄴ	니은 [ni-eun]	ㄴ			
ㄷ	디귿 [di-geut]	ㅡ	ㄷ		
ㄹ	리을 [ri-eul]	ㄱ	ㄱ	ㄹ	
ㅁ	미음 [mi-eum]	ㅣ	ㄲ	ㅁ	
ㅂ	비읍 [bi-eup]	ㅣ	ㅣㅣ	ㅐ	ㅂ
ㅅ	시옷 [si-ot]	ノ	ㅅ		
ㅇ	이응 [i-eung]	ㅇ			
ㅈ	지읒 [ji-eut]	ㄱ	ㅈ		
ㅊ	치읓 [chi-eut]	ㅡ	ㄱ	ㅊ	
ㅋ	키읔 [ki-euk]	ㄱ	ㅋ		
ㅌ	티읕 [ti-eut]	ㅡ	ㅡ	ㅌ	
ㅍ	피읖 [pi-eup]	ㅡ	ㄱ	ㄲ	ㅍ
ㅎ	히읗 [hi-eut]	ㅡ	ㅡ	ㅎ	

Forming Different Syllable Blocks

We have learned the pronunciation of all the vowels and consonants and the characters that represent them. Now, let's study how we can use these characters practically. The minimum unit of Korean writing is called a syllable block. There are four ways to make a syllable block in Korean:

Type 1: Vowel only   아, 어, 오, 우, 이 etc.

Type 2: Vowel + Consonant(s)   안, 영, 원, 울, 않, 없 etc.

Type 3: Consonant + Vowel   가, 너, 로, 배, 화, 쑤 etc.

Type 4: Consonant + Vowel + Consonant(s)   랄, 꽃, 숨, 청, 값 etc.

∗Note

A syllable block beginning with a vowel always has 'ㅇ' in the initial position; however, this 'ㅇ' does not have any phonetic value. The consonant 'ㅇ' only has phonetic value [ng] in the final position, i.e., [ng] sound as in 강 [gang] or 방 [bang].

Phonetic Reading

In this stage, we need to practice reading Korean words phonetically as they are transcribed in the introduction of Korean vowels and consonants. There are a series of phonetic rules in reading Korean words. The rules will be introduced one by one when it is necessary as we progress. The following rules are introduced initially to practice Korean words phonetically:

1) The final consonants, ㄷ, ㅅ, ㅆ, ㅈ, ㅊ, ㅌ, ㅎ are all pronounced as a [t].

Among the consonants, ㄷ, ㅅ, ㅆ, ㅈ, ㅊ, ㅌ, ㅎ are pronounced with their original phonetic values in the initial position of a syllable. However, when they are placed in the final position of a syllable, all these consonants, except ㅌ, lose their original sounds, and they gain the phonetic value of the English [t], but the sound is not released:

갇 [gat]   갓 [gat]   갔 [gat]   갖 [gat]   갗 [gat]   같 [gat]   갛 [gat]

2) As explained in the introduction of Korean consonants, ㄱ and ㅂ are pronounced as [g] and [b]; however, when they are placed in the final position of a syllable, they arepronounced as a [k] sound for ㄱ, and as a [p] sound for ㅂ.

ㄱ [g] or [k]   각 [gak]
ㅂ [b] or [p]   밥 [bap]

Exercise 0:1

Read each syllable in the following chart. Start on row '1' with 'Type 1,' and continue by reading 'Type 2,' 'Type 3' and lastly 'Type 4' for each row.

	Type 1	Type 2	Type 3	Type4
1	아	악	가	값
2	야	않	내	남
3	애	얼	더	닫
4	어	없	레	랄
5	예	옹	모	뮵
6	오	욥	뮤	병
7	요	웃	쇄	선
8	우	웇	쥐	잣
9	유	원	최	춤
10	와	왠	콰	쾅
11	워	웬	튀	튄
12	의	월	프	팝
13	이	잎	히	홀

Phonetic Writing

In this exercise, listen to a sound and transcribe phonetically the sound with Korean characters. Firs, try to to find out the number of syllables, and then transcribe these syllables one by one using Korean characters. The proper steps for the phonetic dictation are as follows:

> 1) Find out how many syllables are in the sound.
>
> 2) Find out which type of Korean syllable (Type 1, 2, 3, 4) it is.
>
> 3) Start to transcribe one syllable at a time, in order.

For instance, the word 사람[sa-ram], consists of two syllables. The first syllable is the Type 3, '사'. The second syllable is the Type 4, '람'. Eventually, you can transcribe the two syllable word as '사람'. Through continuous exercise of this dictation you will be able to transcribe pronunciations of Korean sounds into Korean characters.

Exercise 0:2

The following Korean words have been transcribed in the bracket using our Romanization system. Each syllable is represented by a hyphen. Transcribe the words below into Korean characters. To check how the Korean vowels and consonants are Romanized in our system, please look back at the Introduction of Korean vowels and consonants on page 6. An example has been done below:

e.g., [mo-ja] ⟶ 모자

	Pronunciation	Korean		Pronunciation	Korean
1	[ga-gu]		11	[gol-mok]	
2	[no-ran]		12	[ra-myeon]	
3	[do-jang]		13	[man-du]	
4	[si-gol]		14	[an-gyeong]	
5	[ban-chan]		15	[pa-jeon]	
6	[eo-reum]		16	[hyang-gi]	
7	[jeon-cha]		17	[dal-ryeok]	
8	[a-chim]		18	[sin-mun]	
9	[jeo-nyeok]		19	[gam-ja]	
10	[byeong-won]		20	[pung-sok]	

Names of Hangeul Characters

Now, we're going to learn the names of the Korean characters. Once we know the names of the characters, we can verbally refer to each character, and therefore memorize the spelling of a Korean word.

Vowels do not have separate names, and the pronunciation of a vowel is the name of that character. For example, the vowel 'ㅏ' is pronounced as [a], and it is simply named '아'.

Unlike vowels, Korean consonants have separate names. The following consists of the names of the consonants, so it's necessary to memorize them through reading and writing.

Character	Name	Pronunciation
ㄱ	기역	[gi-yeok]
ㄴ	니은	[ni-eun]
ㄷ	디귿	[di-geut]
ㄹ	리을	[ri-eul]
ㅁ	미음	[mi-eum]
ㅂ	비읍	[bi-eup]
ㅅ	시옷	[si-ot]
ㅇ	이응	[i-eung]
ㅈ	지읒	[ji-eut]
ㅊ	치읓	[chi-eut]
ㅋ	키읔	[ki-euk]
ㅌ	티읕	[ti-eut]
ㅍ	피읖	[pi-eup]
ㅎ	히읗	[hi-eut]

Characteristics of Korean Sentence in Comparison with English.

The following information is just provided for your understanding before you start to learn Korean sentences. As you learn about Korean sentences in your lessons, detailed explanations will be shown with actual examples.

1) The basic word order of a Korean sentence is:

       Subject + Object + Verb.

       She (Subject) + you (Object) + love (Verb).

   The basic order of an English sentence is:

   Subject + Verb + Object.

   She (Subject) + loves (Verb) + you (Object).

2) A subject and/or an object is often omitted when it is understandable in context without it.

3) There are different speech forms depending on who is being addressed:

       (1) Formal Polite   (2) Informal Polite

       (3) Formal Plain   (4) Informal Plain

4) A modifying phrase or clause comes before the noun that is being modified.

       English: He met a person who is studying Korean.

       Korean: He + a (studying Korean) person + met.

5) There is a group of words called 'Particles' or 'Markers,' which are attached to the end of a word to indicate that the word functions as a 'subject marker,' 'object marker,' 'destination marker' etc:

       Subject + (S. Marker) + Object + (O. Marker) + Verb.

6) Due to the role of the above markers, the word order of a Korean sentence is flexible.

A few Expressions for Memorization

The following are a few useful expressions for memorization to practice before you begin to study LESSON 1.

Korean	Pronunciation	English
네. 예.	[ne] [ye]	Yes.
아니요.	[a-ni-yo]	No.
여보세요!	[yeo-bo-se-yo]	Hello!
안녕하세요?	[an-nyeong-ha-se-yo]	Hello? How are you?
안녕히 가세요!	[an-nyeong-hi-ga-se-yo]	Goodbye! (to a person who is leaving)
안녕히 계세요!	[an-nyeong-hi-gye-se-yo]	Goodbye! (to a person who is staying)
처음 뵙겠습니다.	[cheo-eum-boep-get-seum-ni-da]	Pleased to meet you. (for the first time)
좋습니다!	[jot-seum-ni-da]	(It's) good!
실례합니다.	[sil-rye-ham-ni-da]	Excuse me.
감사합니다. 고맙습니다.	[gam-sa-ham-ni-da] [go-map-seum-ni-da]	Thank you.
미안합니다. 죄송합니다.	[mi-an-ham-ni-da] [joe-song-ham-ni-da]	I'm sorry.
천만에요.	[chon-man-e-yo]	You're welcome. Don't mention it.

Structure of Each Lesson

1) Title

2) Situation

3) Dialogue

4) Translation

5) Vocabulary

6) Expressions

7) Grammar Notes

8) Exercises

9) Culture Notes

How to Study Each Lesson

1) Read the dialogue aloud slowly a few times. As in learning any new language, reading aloud is critical.

2) Review the Vocabulary and Expressions sections. Again, read aloud each word several times.

3) Study each dialogue consulting the Grammar Notes and Translations sections.

4) After you understand the dialogue in terms of structure, meaning, and context, repeat the dialogue until you can say it without looking at it.

Using Different Speech Forms

Speakers of the Korean language choose a speech form depending on whom they are addressing. There are basically four different speech forms:

1) Formal Polite
2) Informal Polite
3) Formal Plain
4) Informal Plain

The speaker decides which speech form to use based on the age, social position, and personal relationship to the listener. The speaker initially chooses either the Polite Form or the Plain Form.

Each speech form is subdivided into two forms: Formal Polite vs Informal Polite; Formal Plain and Informal Plain.

In general, Polite Form is used to address an older person or 'senior', and Plain Form is used with a younger person or junior, as well as with intimate friends.

However, in the same level, the speakers often change their speech form between Formal and Informal.

In this text, we are first going to learn various dialogues in Formal Politespeech form because it is the most informative and rigid in structure. Formal Polite is commonly used when we talk to a senior of age or social status, and it is always socially acceptable. For these reasons, once you learn Formal Polite speech form, the other speech forms are relatively simple to learn.

Korean Verbs in Learning Korean as a Second Language

In learning Korean as a second language, Korean verbs are categorized into two groups: Action Verbs and State Verbs.

- Action Verbs are words that describe actions and movements, i.e., 'go,' 'love,' 'study.'
- StateVerbs are words that describe nature and state, i.e., 'good,' 'hot,' 'beautiful.' In this respect, most English adjectives are the equivalent of Korean State Verbs.

The reason that these two groups of words are categorized as 'Verbs' is that, these two groups of words are conjugated in almost the same patterns in Korean.

Other than these two major groups of verbs, there are two sets of special verbs:

- Identification verb: '이다' '아니다'
- Existence/Possession verb: '있다' '없다'

These two special verbs are conjugated somewhat differently in comparison with Action Verbs and State Verbs.

Situation: Jenny and Michael meet for the first time in Korea. They greet each other and tell each other their names and where they are from.

Dialogue

마이클   안녕하십니까?

제니   예, 안녕하십니까?

마이클   처음 뵙겠습니다. 저는 마이클입니다.

제니   반갑습니다. 제 이름은 제니입니다.

마이클   미국 사람입니까?

제니   아니요, 저는 미국 사람이 아닙니다. 저는 캐나다 사람입니다.

마이클   아, 그렇습니까? 반갑습니다.

Translation

Michael	How are you?
Jenny	I'm fine. How are you?
Michael	Nice to meet you. (Lit: I'm seeing you for the first time.) I'm Michael.
Jenny	I'm glad (to meet you). My name is Jenny.
Michael	Are you an American?
Jenny	No, I'm not an American. I'm a Canadian.
Michael	Ah, is that right? Glad to meet you.

NOUN	
저	I
제(저의)	I or my
이름	name
미국	America
사람	person; people
미국 사람	American
캐나다	Canada
캐나다 사람	Canadian

VERB	
안녕하시다	(be) well; to be in good health
뵙다	to see; to meet (an honorific verb)
이다	to be
아니다	not to be
반갑다	(be) glad
그렇다	(be) so

ADVERB	
처음	for the first time

PARTICLE	
은/는	a particle (topic marker)
이/가	a particle (subject marker)

ADDITIONAL VOCABULARY			
한국	Korea	한국 사람	Korean
중국	China	중국 사람	Chinese
일본	Japan	일본 사람	Japanese

Expressions

"예." or "네."	"Yes."
"아니요."	"No."
"안녕하세요?"	Informal Polite form of "안녕하십니까?"
"처음 뵙겠습니다."	"Nice to meet you."
	(Lit: "I'm seeing you for the first time.")
"반갑습니다."	"I'm glad (to meet you)."
"안녕히 계십시오."	"Goodbye!" (to a person who is staying)
"안녕히 가십시오."	"Goodbye!' (to a person who is leaving)

Pronunciation

1) ㅂ is pronounced as [p] in the final position of a syllable, as in 집[jip]. However, it is pronounced as [m] if the initial sound of the nextsyllableis ㄴ[n]:

    ____입[im]니다   ____습[seum]니다   ____님[nim]니다

2) ㄷ, ㅌ, ㅈ, ㅊ, ㅎ, ㅅ, ㅆ are pronounced naturally with their original sounds in the initial position of a syllable, but in the final position of a syllable, they are all pronounced as [t], and it's not released:

    그렇[reot]습니다

Grammar Notes

1) The structure of the sentence "저는 마이클입니다." Is:

   Subject + Particle + Complement + Verb:

   "저(Subject) + 는(Particle) + 마이클(Complement) + 입니다(Verb)."

2) 은/는 is a particle ('topic' marker) attached to the subject of a sentence.

   '은' is attached after a consonant ending: 마이클(Michael)은

   '는' is after a vowel ending: 제니(Jenny)는

3) 이/가 is also a particle ('subject' marker) attached to a subject of a sentence.

   '이' is attached after a consonant ending: 마이클(Michael)이

   '가' is attached to a vowel ending: 제니(Jenny)가

---

*Note
1) We can attach '이/가' or '은/는' after a subject of a sentence; however, we are going to learn
   how to use these two particles in different situations as we learn actual sentences.
2) In case of 'I', 저는 and 제가 is used, not 제는 or 저가

---

4) _____입니다 is an 'Identification Verb (IV)'. The English equivalent of this verb is all 'be'
   verbs (am/are/is). However, unlike English, regardless of first person, second person,
   singular or plural usages, only one form, '_____입니다' is used.

5) '입니다' is an affirmative ending (Statement), and '입니까?' is an interrogative ending
   (Question). (Table 1 in Appendix)

6) A noun + (이/가) 아닙니다 creates a Negative Identification:

   저는 마이클이 아닙니다. (I'm not Michael.)

   저는 제니가 아닙니다. (I'm not Jenny.)

7) _____겠습니다 is a verb ending which is used for the following situations:

   (1) I will.......   저는 가겠습니다. (I'll go.)

   (2) Will you......?   가겠습니까? (Will you go?)

   (3) I guess or assume.......   비가 오겠습니다. (It will rain.)   * 비 rain

Try to say, and then write the following sentences in Korean.

1) I am seeing you for the first time.

2) I am glad to meet you.

3) My name is John(존).

4) Is Michael a Canadian?

5) Yes, he is. (lit. It is so.)

6) Joanne(조앤) is not Japanese.

7) Oh, isn't Joanne Japanese?

8) My name is not Jenny.

9) Is that right?

10) Goodbye! (to a person who is staying)

Situation: Jenny and Thomas talk about people at school.

Dialogue

제니	저 사람은 누구입니까?
토마스	그 사람은 티나입니다.
제니	티나는 이 학교의 학생입니까?
토마스	네, 그렇습니다.
	티나는 대학원 학생입니다.
제니	저 분은 누구입니까?
토마스	그 분은 박 선생님입니다.
	박 선생님은 이 대학교의 교수님입니다.

Translation

Jenny	Who is that person?
Thomas	The person is Tina.
Jenny	Is Tina a student of this school?
Thomas	Yes, she is.
	Tina is a graduate student.
Jenny	Who is that person?
Thomas	The person is Mr. Park.
	Mr. Park is a professor of this university.

Vocabulary

NOUN	
누구	who or whom
학교	a school
학생	a student
대학교	a university
대학원	a graduate school
분	a person (honorific noun of 사람)
박	Park (Korean last name)
선생님	a teacher; Mr.
교수님	a professor

NOUN MODIFIER	
이	this (close to the speaker) 이 사람 (this person)
저	that (away from the speaker and listener) 저 사람 (that person)
그	the (close to the listener or something not present but acknowledged by the listener) 그 사람 (the person)

PARTICLE	
의	Noun + 's

ADDITIONAL VOCABULARY	
대학생	a university student
친구	friend
집	house; home

Grammar Notes

의 is a particle that functions as a possessive marker. In English, it is the same as using the ['s] or [of] to show possession of an object.

그 학교의 교수 (a professor of the school)
제니의 친구　(Jenny's friend)

Translate the following sentences into Korean.

1) Who is that student?

2) Is the person a teacher of this school?

3) Thomas is Jenny's friend.

4) The house is my friend's house.

5) Is Tina(티나) Jenny's friend?

6) No, Tina is not Jenny's friend.

7) The person is not a professor of the university.

8) Is Betty(베티) a student of this graduate school?

9) Is Mr. Park a teacher of that school?

10) No, Mr. Park is not a teacher of that school.

What is that building?

Situation: Jenny and Thomas talk about the buildings on the street.

Dialogue

제니   이것은 무엇입니까?

토마스   이것은 백화점입니다.

제니   저것은 무엇입니까?

토마스   저것은 병원입니다.

         저는 저 병원에서 일합니다.

제니   저 건물도 병원입니까?

토마스   아닙니다. 그것은 병원이 아닙니다.

         그 건물은 시청입니다.

제니   아, 그렇습니까?

         그 건물은 참 좋습니다.

Translation

Jenny	What is this?
Thomas	This is a department store.
Jenny	What is that?
Thomas	That is a hospital.
	I'm working at that hospital.
Jenny	Is that building also a hospital?
Thomas	No, it's not a hospital.
	The building is city hall.
Jenny	Oh, is it?
	The building is very good.

Vocabulary

PRONOUN	이것 this (thing)
	저것 that (thing)
	그것 the (thing); it
	무엇 what; something; anything
NOUN	백화점 a department store
	병원 a hospital
	시청 a city hall
	건물 a building
PARTICLE	도 also: too
VERB	일하다 to work
	좋다 (be) good
ADVERB	참 really: very

Grammar Notes

1) 이것, 저것, 그것 are pronouns referring to things or items depending on the distance between the referent and the speaker and/or the listener :

이것   this (close to the speaker)
저것   that (away from the speaker and listener)
그것   it (close to the listener or understood by the listener)

* 이것, 저것, 그것 cannot be used for referring to a person.

2) _____에서: a particle attached to

   a) (at/in/for) a place where action is happening
      저는 학교에서 공부합니다. (I'm studying at school.)
      마이클은 병원에서 일합니다. (Michel is working for the hospital.)
   b) (from) a place or time
      제니는 학교에서 옵니다. (Jenny is coming from school.)

3) _____도

   a) '도' can be attached to a subject or object, and it means "too" or "also."
   b) When '도' is attached to a subject or object, then the subject marker or object marker should be omitted.
      Example: 저는도   (X)
             저도 갑니다.   (O)
             (I am going too.)
             중국말을도   (X)
             저는 중국말도 공부합니다.   (O)
             (I study Chinese language also.)

Exercise 3

Translate the following sentences into Korean.

1)   What is that building?

2)   It is a university.

3)   I'm working at City Hall.

4)   Is that also a hospital?

5)   It is not a hospital.

6)   Isn't it a department store?

7)   Is the building Jenny's school?

8)   I'm working at the building.

9)   Is the department store very good?

10)   Is Jenny also working at City Hall?

What are you doing?

Situation: Jenny and Michael talk about what they are doing in Korea.

Dialogue

마이클	한국에서 무엇을 하십니까?
제니	한국말을 공부합니다.
마이클	어디에서 한국어를 공부합니까?
제니	하나 대학교에서 공부합니다.
마이클	아, 그렇습니까?
	저도 하나 대학교에서 한국 역사를 공부합니다.
제니	오늘도 학교에 가십니까?
마이클	아니요, 학교에 가지 않습니다.
	저는 오늘 시내에 갑니다.
제니	아, 저도 시내에 갑니다.
마이클	그럼, 같이 갑시다.

Translation

Michael	What are you doing in Korea?
Jenny	I'm studying the Korean language.
Michael	Where are you studying Korean?
Jenny	I'm studying at Hana University.
Michael	Oh, are you?
	I'm also studying Korean history at Hana University.
Jenny	Do you go to school today too?
Michael	No, I don't go to school.
	I'm going to downtown today.
Jenny	Oh, I'm also going downtown.
Michael	Then, let's go together.

1) When a proceeding ㄱ is directly connected to the initial consonant of next syllable, the consonant is pronounced as a stressed double consonant

　　학교　[hak-kkyo] not [hak-gyo]

　　식당　[sik-ttang] not [sik-dang]

2) The adverb 같이 (together) is pronounced as [gat-chi] according to a phonetic rule.

Vocabulary

NOUN	
	학교　a school
	대학교　a university
	('하나') 대학교　('Hana') university
	한국　Korea
	한국말 / 한국어　Korean language
	역사　history
	한국 역사　Korean history
	오늘　today
	시내　downtown; (within, inside) the city

PRONOUN	어디 where
	a) 어디에 to where (destination)
	b) 어디에서 at/in where (place where action takes)
	c) 어디에서 from where

VERB	하다 to do
	공부하다 to study
	가다 to go

ADVERB	같이 together
	그럼 if so; in that case; then (shorten form of 그러면)

PARTICLE	_____에서 (a) at / in (b) from
	_____을 / 를 a particle attached to an object
	_____에 to (a destination)

ADDITIONAL VOCABULARY	중국어 / 중국말 Chinese language
	일본어 / 일본말 Japanese language
	영어 English
	어제 yesterday
	내일 tomorrow
	지금 now
	언제 when
	식당 a restaurant
	오다 to come

1) Korean verbs regularly change their form depending on situations and contexts. The changing of a verb form is called the 'verb conjugation.' To conjugate verbs properly, we have to know some basic concepts of Korean verbs.

   Take the verb 'to go (가다)' for instance.
   '가다' is called 'Basic Form' or 'Dictionary Entry Form (DEF)' of the verb.

   The basic form of a verb consists of two parts: a 'Verb Stem' and a' Verb Ending.' The basic form of all Korean verbs end with '다.'

   The stem is the remaining part, the part without '다'. So the stem of '가다' is '가', and '다' is a verb ending.

2) The following formula is the verb ending to make an Affirmative statement (Appendix 1: Table 1).

   (a) ______ㅂ니다 (stem ends in a vowel)
   　　가다　〉　갑니다
   　　오다　〉　옵니다
   (b) ______습니다 (stem ends in a consonant)
   　　잡다　〉　잡습니다
   　　반갑다　〉　반갑습니다
   　　그렇다　〉　그렇습니다

3) The verb ending of a question (Interrogative ending) is simply made by changing the verb ending of a statement 다 into 까? (Appendix 1: Table 1).

   　　갑니다　〉　갑니까?　(Do you go?)
   　　옵니다　〉　옵니까?　(Do you come?)
   　　잡습니다　〉　잡습니까?　(Do you catch?)
   　　반갑습니다　〉　반갑습니까?　(Are you glad?)
   　　그렇습니다　〉　그렇습니까?　(Is it right?)

4) ______(으)십시오 is a verb ending used to make a Command or request (Appendix 1: Table 1).

   ______십시오 is attached to a verb stem that ends in a vowel,

_____(으)십시오 is attached to a stem that ends in a consonant.

가 + 십시오 〉 가십시오 (please go)

잡 + 으십시오 〉 잡으십시오 (please catch)

5) In Korean, it is very important that you show respect properly to your seniors or elders. Thus, in order to show respect to a subject of a sentence, a speaker adds an honorific stem to the original stem. It is called 'Honorific.' '시' is added after a vowel of the stem, '으시' after a consonant of the stem (Appendix 2: Honorific Expressions).

a) 가다   가 + 시 + ㅂ니다 〉 가십니다

b) 잡다   잡 + 으시 + ㅂ니다 〉 잡으십니다

However, there are some verbs which have completely different Honorific verbs. In that case, those Honorific verbs must be used instead of adding 시 or 으시 to the original verbs.

i.e. 있다 〉 계시다

6) _____을/를: a particle attached to the object in the sentence

a) 을 after consonant ending: 마이클(Michael)을

b) 를 after vowel ending: 제니(Jenny)를

7) _____에: a particle for a destination (a place to go or to come)

8) _____지 않습니다: verb ending for a negative statement in the present tense: a long negation (Appendix 1: Table 1).

하지 않습니다 (not to do) / 가지 않습니다 (not to go)

9) 안 + statement/question: another form of negation: a short negation (Appendix 1: Table 1).

안 갑니다 (don't go)   안 갑니까? (don't you go?)

10) _____ㅂ시다 / _____읍시다: verb ending for a proposal (Appendix 1: Table 1).

a) _____ㅂ시다 is for vowel endings: 갑시다 (Let's go.)

b) _____읍시다 is for a consonant endings: 삽읍시다 (Let's catch it.)

Translate the following sentences into Korean.

1)   Where are you going now? (Honorific)

2)   I'm going to school.

3)   What are you studying at university?

4)   I'm studying the Korean Language.

5)   Do you study Korean history as well?

6)   No, I don't study Korean history now.

7)   Where do you study English?

8)   I don't go downtown today.

9)   What are you doing tomorrow? (Honorific)

10)   Then, let's study at school together tomorrow.

Where did you come from?

Situation: Jenny meets Asako in Korea for the first time.

Dialogue

제니　실례지만, 어디에서 오셨습니까?

아사코　일본에서 왔습니다.

제니　언제 한국에 오셨습니까?

아사코　금년 5월에 왔습니다.

제니　수잔도 일본에서 왔습니까?

아사코　아니요, 수잔은 일본에서 오지 않았습니다.

제니　그럼, 수잔은 어느 나라에서 왔습니까?

아사코　중국에서 왔습니다.

　　　수잔과 저는 한국에 와서 처음 만났습니다.

Translation

Jenny　Excuse me, where are you come from?

Asako　I came from Japan.

Jenny　When did you come to Korea?

Asako　I came in May of this year.

Jenny　Did Susan also come from Japan?

Asako　No, Susan didn't come from Japan.

Jenny　Then, which country did Susan come from?

Asako　She came from China.

　　　Susan and I came to Korea and met for the first time.

Vocabulary

NOUN	언제　when 금년　the current year 나라　a country 월　month 　　일월(1월: January), 이월(2월: February), 삼월(3월: March) 　　사월(4월: April), 오월(5월: May), 유월(6월: June), 칠월(7월: July), 팔월(8월: August), 구월(9월: September), 시월(10월: October), 십일월(11월: November), 십이월(12월: December)
VERB	오다　to come 만나다　to meet
ADVERB	처음　for the first time
PARTICLE	1) _____에서 　a) from (a place or time) 　　저는 중국에서 왔습니다. (I came from China.) 　b) at / in 　　저는 학교에서 공부합니다. (I'm studying at school.) 　　제니는 중국에서 공부합니다. (Jenny is studying in China.) 2) _____에 　a) at / in (time marker) 　b) to (destination marker) 　　3월에 한국에 왔습니다. (I came to Korea in March.) 3) _____와(과)　(Noun) and (Noun) 　a) 제니와 마이클　Jenny and Michael 　b) 마이클과 제니　Michael and Jenny

<table>
<tr><td>NOUN MODIFIER</td><td>어느　which: 어느 학교 (which school)

어느 사람 (which person)</td></tr>
</table>

<table>
<tr><td>ADDITIONAL VOCABULARY</td><td>일　date
1일(일일), 2일(이일), 3일(삼일), 4일(사일), 5일(오일), 6일(육일)⋯

작년　last year
내년　next year
사랑하다　to love</td></tr>
</table>

Sino-Korean Numbers / Korean Numbers

1	2	3	4	5	6	7	8	9	10
일	이	삼	사	오	육	칠	팔	구	십
하나	둘	셋	넷	다섯	여섯	일곱	여덟	아홉	열

11	12	13	14	15	16	17	18	19	20
십일	십이	십삼	십사	십오	십육	십칠	십팔	십구	이십
열하나	열둘	열셋	열넷	열다섯	열여섯	열일곱	열여덟	열아홉	스물

※ 100(백)　1,000(천)　10,000(만)

Grammar Notes

1) Verb ending of the Affirmative (Positive) Past Tense is expressed in the structure, _____(았, 었, 였)습니다 (Appendix 1: Table 1).

   a) _____았습니다 after a stem with a vowel '아' or '오':

      가 + 았습니다 〉 갔습니다 (went)

      오 + 았습니다 〉 왔습니다 (came)*

      잡 + 았습니다 〉 잡았습니다 (caught)

* When a vowel is directly connected to the initial vowel of next syllable, it is often contracted in a syllable: 오 + 았 〉 왔

   b) _____었습니다 after a stem with a vowel '어', '우', '으', '이'

      먹 + 었습니다 〉 먹었습니다 (ate)

      집 + 었습니다 〉 집었습니다 (picked up)

   c) _____였습니다 after a verb of which basic form ends with '하다'

      ('하다 verbs')

      하 + 였습니다 〉 했습니다 (did)*

      공부하 + 였습니다 〉 공부했습니다 (studied)

        * '하였' is usually contracted as '했' in conversations.

2) Honorific '시' + '었습니다,' should usually be contracted as 셨습니다.

3) '와'/'과' is a particle connecting a noun and a noun. It means 'and.'
   '와' is attached when preceding noun ends in a vowel, and
   '과' is attached after a consonant:

   a) 제니와 마이클 (Jenny and Michael)
   b) 마이클과 제니 (Michael and Jenny)

4) '_____지 않았습니다' is formula for verb ending for Negative Past Tense (Appendix 1: Table 1).

   가지 않았습니다 (didn't go)   잡지 않았습니다 (didn't catch)

5) 안 + statement/question: another form of negation (a short negation)

   안 갔습니다 (didn't go)   안 갔습니까? (didn't you go?)

6) Korean uses two numerical systems: Korean numbers and Sino-Korean numbers. We are going to learn the different usages of these two systems one by one with actual examples.

   Sino-Korean numbers:
   1(일), 2(이), 3(삼), 4(사), 5(오), 6(육), 7(칠), 8(팔), 9(구), 10(십)
   11(십일), 12(십이)......20(이십)......100(백) 1,000(천) 10,000(만)

7) _____(아/어/여)서

   a) This connective verb suffix is used to show a sequence of directly connected actions.
   학교에 가서 공부했습니다. (I went to school and studied.)

   b) It is also used to show a reason of the following action, state or situation.
   비가 와서 가지 않았습니다. (It was raining so I didn't go.)

   c) This suffix is used in a statement or a question, not in a command or a proposal.

Exercise 5

Translate the following sentences into Korean.

1) Didn't you meet the person in England?

2) Which person did you meet last year? (Honorific)

3) Which country did you come from? (Honorific)

4) Who loved Susan?

5) Whom did Susan love?

6) Don't you meet the person at school today?

7) Michael and Jenny came to school for the first time.

8) Jenny did not come from China.

9) I went to the hospital and met the person.

10) When did you come to Canada from Korea?

Shall we go to see a movie?

Situation: Michael and Tina talk on the phone and make plans to go to see a movie.

Dialogue

마이클　티나씨, 오늘 바쁘십니까?

티나　아니요, 바쁘지 않습니다.

마이클　그럼, 저녁에 시간이 있습니까?

티나　네, 시간이 있습니다.

마이클　저녁에 영화를 보러 같이 가겠습니까?

티나　네, 좋습니다.

마이클　지금 몇 시입니까?

티나　3시 30분입니다.

마이클　그럼, 두 시간 후에 카페테리아에서 만납시다.

티나　좋습니다.

Translation

Michael	Tina, are you busy today?
Tina	No, I'm not busy.
Michael	Then, do you have some time in the evening?
Tina	Yes, I do.
Michael	Will you go to watch a movie together in the evening?
Tina	Yes, sounds good.
Michael	What time is it now?
Tina	It's three thirty.
Michael	Then, let's meet at the cafeteria after two hours.
Tina	That's good.

Vocabulary

NOUN	저녁 evening 시간 time; hour 시 o'clock 분 a minute (of an hour) 영화 a movie 후 after 몇 how much; how many (a noun modifier) 카페테리아 a cafeteria
VERB	보다 to see, to watch 만나다 to meet 바쁘다 (be) busy 좋다 (be) good 있다 to have (possession) / to be (existence)
PARTICLE	_____에 a particle attached to: 1) time 2) destination 3) location
ADDITIONAL VOCABULARY	극장 a theatre 영화관 a movie theatre 예쁘다 pretty

Korean Numbers:

1(하나), 2(둘), 3(셋), 4(넷), 5(다섯), 6(여섯), 7(일곱), 8(여덟), 9(아홉), 10(열) 11(열하나), 12(열둘)…20(스물)… 100(백) 1,000(천) 10,000(만)

없다 not to have (possession) or not to be (existence)
'없다' is the negative verb of '있다'.

전   before   후   after
a) 두 시 전(에)   before 2 o'clock
b) 두 시 후(에)   after 2 o'clock

"지금 몇 시입니까?"   "What time is it now?"

Grammar Notes

1) 씨 can be attached after a full name, last name, or first name. However, unless it is an official situation, the use of 씨 to a senior is not appropriate.

2) Noun(이 / 가)   있다 / 없다

   a) to have (possession) / not to have
      시간이 있습니다. (I have time.)
      시간이 없습니다. (I don't have time.)
   b) to be (existence) / not to be
      제니가 학교에 있습니다. (Jenny is at school.)
      제니가 학교에 없습니다. (Jenny is not at school.)

3) '＿＿＿(으)러 가다 / 오다' This structure means 'to go or to come to do something'
   The structure is used only with 가다 and 오다 verbs and no other verbs.

4) ＿＿＿ㅂ시다 / ＿＿＿읍시다 is verb ending for Propositive Ending (Appendix 1: Table 1).
   ＿＿＿ㅂ시다 is attached after a vowel: 가 + ㅂ시다 > 갑시다. (Let's go.)
   ＿＿＿읍시다 is attached after a consonant: 잡 + 읍시다 > 잡읍시다. (Let's catch it.)

5) When Korean numbers are followed by a counting unit, '하나(1)' '둘(2)' '셋(3)' '넷(4)' are changed as modifying forms: '한(1)' '두(2)' '세(3)' '네(4)'

하나 〉 한 + 사람 (one person)
둘 〉 두 + 사람 (two persons)
셋 〉 세 + 사람 (three persons)
넷 〉 네 + 사람 (four persons)

However, from '다섯(5)', the form does not change:

다섯 〉 다섯 + 사람　　　여섯 〉 여섯 + 사람

6) Reading time: Korean numbers are used to read hourly units, and Sino-Korean numbers are for minute units:

(1 : 25) 한 시 이십오 분　　　(2 : 19) 두 시 십구 분

* '시' o'clock / '분' minute(s)

7) 바쁘다 is a State verb and it's a type of Irregular verbs called '으' irregular verb (Appendix 3: Honorific Expressions).

In case of '으' Irregular Verbs,

(1) '—' is omitted before a vowel and replaced with either ㅏ or ㅓ depending on the vowel of the preceding syllable.

(a) If the vowel is 'ㅏ' or 'ㅗ', the omitted '—' becomes 'ㅏ':
바쁘다 〉 바쁘 + 았습니다 〉 바빴습니다

(b) If the vowel is 'ㅓ' 'ㅜ' or '—' 'ㅣ', it becomes 'ㅓ':
예쁘다 〉 예쁘 + 었습니다 〉 예뻤습니다

Exercise 6:1

Read and then write the following times into Korean.

1) 03 : 35 　　　　　　시 　　　　　　분

2) 07 : 28 　　　　　　시 　　　　　　분

3) 08 : 46 　　　　　　시 　　　　　　분

4) 12 : 12 　　　　　　시 　　　　　　분

5) 11 : 05 　　　　　　시 　　　　　　분

6) 05 : 20 　　　　　　시 　　　　　　분

7) 01 : 17 　　　　　　시 　　　　　　분

8) 09 : 31 　　　　　　시 　　　　　　분

9) 04 : 59 　　　　　　시 　　　　　　분

10) 06 : 11 　　　　　　시 　　　　　　분

Exercise 6:2

Translate the following sentences in Korean.

1) Do you have some time tomorrow?

2) I'm very busy tomorrow.

3) When did you go to see a movie?

4) I don't have any time today.

5) Shall we go to City Hall to meet the person?

6) Let's meet at my house tomorrow.

7) I didn't have time yesterday evening.

8) Let's meet at school before 5 o'clock today.

9) Then, shall we meet after one hour?

10) Yes, let's study together at school.

Where is the department store?

Situation: Michael is asking a person about the buildings on the street.

Dialogue

마이클　실례지만, 가나은행이 어디에 있습니까?

행인　가나은행은 바로 저기에 있습니다.

마이클　아, 그렇습니까?

　　　코리아호텔은 어디에 있습니까?

행인　저 가나은행 뒤에 있습니다.

마이클　그러면, 서울백화점도 이 근처에 있습니까?

행인　예, 서울백화점은 코리아호텔 옆에 있습니다.

마이클　대단히 고맙습니다.

행인　천만에요.

Translation

Michael　Excuse me, where is the Gana Bank?

Passerb　The Gana Bank is just over there.

Michael　Oh, is it?

　　　Where is the Korea Hotel?

Passerby　It is behind that Gana Bank.

Michael　Then, is the Seoul Department Store also near here?

Passerby　Yes, the Seoul Department Store is beside the Korea Hotel.

Michael　Thank you very much.

Passerby　You are welcome.

NOUN	가나은행 GanaBank
	저기 over there
	호텔 a hotel
	뒤 behind
	옆 beside; by
	근처 vicinity; near
	백화점 a department store
	서울 Seoul

VERB	고맙다 (be) thankful

ADVERB	바로 just
	대단히 very much

ADDITIONAL VOCABULARY	여기 a place (spot) near the speaker
	저기 a place (spot) away from a speaker and listener
	거기 a place (spot) near the listener or the place understandable in the context.
	앞 front
	아래 below
	위 above
	오른쪽 right side
	왼쪽 left side

Grammar Notes

_____에 a particle attached to   a) time   b) destination   c) location

_____에 있다 / 없다 is used to express a person or an object exists at a place (location):

(그 사람은) 지금 한국에 있습니다. (The person is in Korea now.)
(그 학교는) 서울에 있습니다. (The school is in Seoul.)

Translate the following sentences into Korean.

1) Where are you now?

2) I'm at Korea Hotel.

3) Is the hotel behind the department store?

4) The university is near here.

5) Were you at home at 9 o'clock?

6) I was not at home yesterday evening.

7) Please come here again tomorrow.

8) The building is on the right side of the hospital.

9) Let's go to the place together.

10) Thank you very much!

Situation: Betty and James meet on the street.

Dialogue

제임스 오늘 날씨가 좋아요.

베티 예, 어제 날씨도 참 좋았어요.

제임스 요즈음 어떻게 지내세요?

베티 잘 지냅니다.

제임스 지금 어디에 가세요?

베티 남대문 시장에 갑니다.

제임스 남대문 시장을 좋아하세요?

베티 예, 아주 좋아합니다.

제임스 저는 지금 학교에 가요.

베티 아, 그래요?

  안녕히 가세요!

제임스 예, 나중에 또 봐요.

James	The weather is good today.
Betty	Yes, yesterday's weather was also really nice.
James	How are you doing these days?
Betty	I'm doing well.
James	Where are you going?
Betty	I'm going to Namdaemoon market.
James	Do you like Namdaemoon market?
Betty	Yes, I like it very much.
James	I'm going to school now.
Betty	Oh, is that right?
	Good bye!
James	Yes, See you again later!

Vocabulary

NOUN	날씨 weather
	시장 a market
	'남대문 시장' Namdaemoon ('South Gate') Market

VERB	지내다 to spend time; to get along
	보다 to see; to watch
	좋다 (be) good
	좋아하다 to like

ADVERB	참 really; truely
	요즈음 these days
	어떻게 how
	잘 well
	아주 very (much)
	나중에 later

Expressions

"그래요?"   (Is that right?)

This is the Informal Polite form of '그렇습니까?'

Grammar Notes

1) As previously explained, Korean verbs can be divided into two groups: Action Verbs (AV) and State Verbs (SV). The AVs are the verbs of actions and movement, where-as the SVs are the verbs that describe a nature or state. In English, adjectives are usually considered equivalent to Korean SVs.

   Korean AVs and SVs conjugate the same way in almost all speech forms (Appendix 1: Table 1, 2, 4), the only exception being Formal Plain (Appendix 1: Table 5).

   While we make statements, questions, commands and proposals with AVs, we never make commands or proposals with SVs.

   And, special verbs, 이다 / 아니다 (Identification) and 있다 / 없다 (Possession / Existence) are conjugated in different structures.

2) 좋다 is a state verb which is used with a subject (marker).
   좋아하다 is an action verb which requires an object (marker):

   a) 그 학교가 아주 좋습니다. (The school is very good.)
   b) 저는 그 학교를 아주 좋아합니다. (I like the school very much.)

3) _____(아, 어, 여)요 is a verb ending used for Action verbs when making a statement, question, proposal (only AVs) or command (only AVs) in Informal Polite speech form. Their different functions are naturally understood in actual contexts (Appendix 1: Table 2).

   a) _____아요: after a stem with a vowel '아' or '오':
   가 + 아요 〉 가요
   오 + 아요 〉 와요
   좋 + 아요 〉 좋아요
   잡 + 아요 〉 잡아요

   b) _____어요: after a stem with a vowel '어', '우', '으', '이'
   먹 + 어요 〉 먹어요
   집 + 어요 〉 집어요

c) _____여요: after a verb of which basic form ends with '하다'
('하다 verbs')

하 + 여요 〉 해요

공부하 + 여요 〉 공부해요

4) _____(았, 었, 였)어요 is a verb ending that indicates past tense in Informal Polite. Depending on the context, it can be a statement, question, proposal or command,

가 + 았어요 〉 갔어요

집 + 었어요 〉 집었어요

In case of '하다' verbs, '하였' is usually contracted as '했'.

공부하였 + 어요 〉 공부했어요

일하였 + 어요 〉 일했어요

5) We have learned how to make honorific expressions by adding '시' or '으시'. However, in the case of Informal Polite used in the Present Positive tense, '(으)세요' is used for an honorific verb ending.

a) '_____'세요' is attached after a vowel ending:

공부하 + 세요 〉 공부하세요

b) '_____' 으세요' after a consonant ending:

잡 + 으세요 〉 잡으세요

Change the following sentences into the Informal Polite speech form.

e.g., 한국말을 공부합니까? ⟶ 한국말을 공부해요?

1) 그 사람은 언제 옵니까?

2) 어디에서 한국말을 공부했습니까?

3) 지금 저는 학교에 있습니다.

4) 내일 시장에 가십시오.

5) 지금 은행에 갑시다.

6) 언제 한국에 오셨습니까?

7) 지금 아주 바쁩니까?

8) 지금 바쁘지 않습니다.

9) 오늘 시간이 있습니까?

10) 그럼, 같이 갑시다.

What is your hobby?

Situation: Tom and Jenny talk about their hobbies.

Dialogue

탐	취미가 무엇입니까?
제니	제 취미는 음악 감상입니다.
탐	어떤 음악을 좋아하세요?
제니	저는 모든 음악을 좋아해요.
	특히 재즈 음악이 좋아요.
제니	탐의 취미는 무엇입니까?
탐	저는 모든 운동을 좋아해요.
	특히 권투를 좋아합니다.
	제니도 권투를 좋아하세요?
제니	아니요, 저는 권투를 별로 좋아하지 않아요.

Translation

Tom	What's your hobby?
Jenny	My hobby is listening to music.
Tom	What kind of music do you like?
James	I like all music.
	Jazz music is especially good.
Jenny	What's your hobby, Tom?
Tom	I like all sports.
	I especially like boxing.
	Jenny, do you also like boxing?
Jenny	No, I don't like boxing very much.

Vocabulary

NOUN		
	취미	a hobby
	음악	music
	감상	appreciation of music '음악감상' or appreication of movies '영화감상'
	재즈	jazz
	운동	exercise / sports
	권투	boxing

NOUN MODIFIER		
	어떤	what kinds of; which
	모든	all

ADVERB		
	특히	especially; particularly
	별로	not really; not so much

1) The position of adverbs is very flexible.

'특히' 저는 권투를 좋아해요.
저는 '특히' 권투를 좋아해요.
저는 권투를 '특히' 좋아해요.

2) ______지 않아요 is negation of Informal Polite in present tense. (Table 2 in Appendix)

제니는 시장에 가지 않아요. (Jenny does not go to a market.)
저는 그것을 먹지 않아요. (I don't eat it.)

3) ______지 않았어요 is negation of Informal Polite in past tense.

가 + 지 않았어요 ＞ 가지 않았어요 (didn't go)
오 + 지 않았어요 ＞ 오지 않았어요 (didn't come)

4) The adverb '별로' is used in negative contexts.

그것은 별로 좋지 않아요. (It is not that good.)
저는 그것을 별로 좋아하지 않아요. (I don't like it so much.)

Write the following sentences into Informal Polite.

1) Which sports do you especially like?

2) What kinds of work are you doing now? (Honorific)

3) This market is very good.

4) The weather was not that good yesterday.

5) Do you like all sports? (Honorific)

6) Don't you go to school today?

7) John didn't work at the bank.

8) I didn't like the work so much.

9) I liked the person very much.

10) All schools are good.

Situation: Joan and Terry talk about going out for lunch. The speech form of Lesson 10 is Informal Polite (Appendix Table 2), Lesson 11 is Informal Plain (Appendix Table 4).

Dialogue

테리	아이고, 벌써 1시가 되었어요.
	조앤, 점심 먹었어요?
조앤	아니요, 아직 안 먹었어요.
테리	저는 아주 배고파요!
조앤	저도 그래요.
	같이 밥 먹으러 가요.
테리	어느 식당에 갈까요?
	국수집에 갈까요? 불고기집에 갈까요?
조앤	무척 배고프니까, 불고기집에 가요.
테리	좋아요, 빨리 가요.

Translation

Terry	Oh my gosh! It's 1 o'clock already.
	Joan, did you eat lunch?
Joan	No, I didn't.
Terry	I'm very hungry!
Joan	So am I.
	Let's go eat together.
Terry	Which restaurant shall we go to?
	Shall we go to a noodle house? Or a bulgogi house?
Joan	Since we are very hungry, let's go to a bulgogi house.
Terry	Sounds good. Let's go quickly.

Vocabulary

NOUN	밥 1) a meal 2) cooked rice 국수 + 집 〉 국수집 a noodle-house 불고기 + 집 〉 불고기집 a bugogi-house 점심 lunch; luncheon
VERB	되다 to become 먹다 to eat 배고프다 (be) hungry
ADVERB	벌써 already 빨리 quickly; fast 아직 yet 아주 / 무척 very much
ADDITIONAL VOCABULARY	집다 to pick up 슬프다 (be) sad

Expressions

"아이고!" is a common exclamatory expression of Korean, meaning 'Oh my gosh!'

"배가 고픕니다 (or 배고픕니다) / 배가 고파요(or 배고파요)." "I'm hungry."

Grammar Notes

1) '안 + statement or question' is called a short negation, while a long negation is expressed in '_____지 않습니다 (Formal Polite)' or '_____지 않아요' (Informal Polite).

    a) 안 + statement / question: another form of negation (short negation)
      안 가요 (don't go)   안 가요? (don't you go?)
    b) 안 + statement / question: another form of negation (short negation)
      안 갔어요 (didn't go)   안 갑니까? (didn't you go?)

2) _____(았, 었, 였)어요 is the verb ending for a statement or a question, in the past tense for Informal Polite speech (Appendix 1: Table 2).

    a) _____았어요: after a stem with a vowel '아' or '오':
      가 + 았어요 〉 갔어요
      오 + 았어요 〉 왔어요

    b) _____었어요: after a stem with a vowel '어', '우', '으', '이'
      먹 + 었어요 〉 먹었어요 (ate)
      집 + 었어요 〉 집었어요 (picked up)

    c) _____였어요 after a verb of which basic form ends with '하다' ('하다 verbs')
      하 + 였어요 〉 했어요
      공부하 + 였어요〉 공부했어요

4) 배고프다 is a type of irregular verbs called '으' irregular verb (Appendix 3: Irregular Verbs).

    'ㅡ' is omitted before a vowel and replaced with either ㅏ or ㅓ depending on the vowel of the preceding syllable.

    (a) If the vowel is 'ㅏ' or 'ㅗ', add 'ㅏ':
      배고프다 〉 배고프 + 아요 〉 배고파요
    (b) If the vowel is 'ㅓ' 'ㅜ' or 'ㅡ' 'ㅣ', add 'ㅓ':
      슬프다 〉 슬프 + 어요 〉 슬퍼요

5) 4) _____(으)ㄹ까요?   This verb ending is used for

    a) a proposal: 같이 갈까요? (Shall we go together?)
    b) possibility in question: 그 사람이 올까요? (Will he come?)
    c) in Formal polite, "(으)ㄹ까요?" is usually expressed as _____겠습니까?

Change the dialogue of Lesson 10 into Formal Polite.

테리 아이고, 벌써 1시가 되었어요.

　　　조앤, 점심 먹었어요?

조앤 아니요, 아직 안 먹었어요.

테리 저는 아주 배고파요!

조앤 저도 그래요.

　　　같이 밥 먹으러 가요.

테리 어느 식당에 갈까요?

　　　국수집에 갈까요? 불고기집에 갈까요?

조앤 무척 배고프니까, 불고기집에 가요.

테리 좋아요, 빨리 가요.

Let's go out for Lunch (2)

Situation: Joan and Terry talk about going out for lunch. The speech form of Lesson 10 is Informal Polite (Appendix 1: Table 2), Lesson 11 is Informal Plain (Appendix 1: Table 4).

Dialogue

테리	아이고, 벌써 1시가 되었어.
	조앤, 점심 먹었어?
조앤	아니, 아직 안 먹었어.
테리	나는 아주 배고파!
조앤	나도 그래.
	같이 밥 먹으러 가.
테리	어느 식당에 갈까?
	국수집에 갈까? 불고기집에 갈까?
조앤	무척 배고프니까, 불고기집에 가.
테리	좋아, 빨리 가.

Translation

Terry	Oh my gosh! It's 1 o'clock already.
	Joan, did you eat lunch?
Joan	No, I didn't.
Terry	I'm very hungry!
Joan	So am I.
	Let's go to eat together.
Terry	Which restaurant shall we go to?
	Shall we go to a noodle house? Or a bulgogi house?
Joan	Since we are very hungry hungry, let's go to a bulgogi house.
Terry	Sounds good. Let's go quickly.

Vocabulary and Expressions

Same as Lesson 10

나 'I' (in plain speech form)

Grammar Notes

1) _____(아, 어, 여) is the verb ending for a statement, a question, a command, and a proposal in present tense for Informal Plain speech.

   a) _____아: after a stem with a vowel '아' or '오'
   가 + 아 〉 가.
   오 + 아 〉 와.

   b) _____어: after a stem with a vowel '어', '우', '으', '이'
   먹 + 어 〉 먹어.
   집 + 어 〉 집어.

   c) _____여: after a verb of which basic form ends with '하다' ("하다 verbs")
   하 + 여 〉 해.
   공부하 + 여 〉 공부해.

2) As indicated in the vocabulary section above, in plain speech form we cannot use '저는' or '제가' for 'I,' instead '나는' or '내가' must be used. However, '나는' and '내가' can be used in polite style if it is acceptable in the context.

Exercise 11

Translate the following sentences into Korean in the speech form indicated in the bracket:

Formal Polite (1)	Informal Polite (2)	Informal Plain (4)

1) Let's go to Korea to study Korean language. (2)

2) Because the person is busy today, please meet him tomorrow. (4)

3) I went there quickly to meet my friend. (1)

4) Shall we meet Mr. Pak(박) together? (2)

5) I was so hungry at school. (1)(배고프다 : '으' irregular verb)

6) At which school did you study? (2)

7) Shall we eat noodles? Shall we eat bulgogi? (4)

8) What kind of sports did you like? (1)

9) I especially liked the department store. (2)

10) The bank is behind the restaurant. (4)

Situation: Nancy is looking for a sports cap at a store. This is a dialogue between Nancy and a clerk.

Dialogue

점원 어서 오십시오!

무엇을 찾으십니까?

낸시 운동모자가 있어요?

점원 네, 여기에 여러 가지 운동 모자가 있습니다.

이건 어떻습니까?

낸시 괜찮은데요.

파란색은 없어요?

점원 파란색은 지금 없습니다.

초록색은 어떻습니까?

낸시 초록색도 좋아요.

신발은 어디에 있어요?

점원 신발은 저기에 있습니다.

Clerk	Please come in!
	What are you looking for?
Nancy	Do you have a sports cap?
Clerk	Yes, we have various sports caps here.
	How is this?
Nancy	Looks okay.
	Don't you have a blue one?
Clerk	We don't have a blue one now.
	How about a green one?
Nancy	The green one is okay too.
	Where are shoes?
Clerk	The shoes are over there.

Vocabulary

NOUN		
	운동	(physical) exercise; sports
	모자	a cap: a hat
	여기	here
	가지	kinds of: sorts of
	파란색	blue color
	초록색	green color

NOUN MODIFIER		
	여러	many: various*
	여러 가지	all sorts (of); various kinds (of)

VERB	찾다 1) to look for
	2) to find out (in the past tense form)
	운동하다 to take exercise
	괜찮다 (be) all right; not so bad

ADVERB	어서 quickly; fast; without delay

ADDITIONAL VOCABULARY	저기 over there (a place away from speaker and listener)
	거기 the place (a place near the listener or a place understandable)
	신발 shoes
	우리 we: our
	노란색 yellow color

Expressions

"어서 오세요!"	"Welcome!" (Informal Polite)
"여기 있어요!"	"Here you are!" (Informal Polite)

Grammar Notes

1) 이건 is a contracted form of 이것은.

2) 'SV_____ㄴ데요 / 은데요' is a verb ending used to explain the situation with a state verb (SV). It can be translated as 'while it is,''since it is' ...... etc.

Exercise 12

Translate the following sentences in Formal Polite.

1) Are you looking for a sports cap?

2) How about that blue cap?

3) Where are sports caps?

4) We don't have green shoes.

5) Whom are you looking for?

6) The person is over there.

7) The blue building is a hospital.

8) Do you have blue caps?

9) No, I don't have a blue cap.

10) We have various shoes.

Situation: This is continuation of Lesson 12.

Dialogue

낸시 　이 모자는 얼마입니까?

점원 　칠천 원입니다.

낸시 　저 셔츠는 얼마예요?

점원 　이만 팔천 원입니다.

낸시 　너무 비싼데요.

　　　좀 싸게 해 주세요.

점원 　그럼……, 이만육천 원만 주세요.

낸시 　모두 얼마입니까?

점원 　음……, 모두 삼만삼천 원이에요.

낸시 　여기 사만 원이 있습니다.

점원 　고맙습니다.

　　　여기 거스름돈 칠천 원이 있습니다.

Nancy	How much is this hat?
Clerk	It's 7,000 won.
Nancy	How much is that shirt?
Clerk	It's 28,000 won.
Nancy	It's too expensive.
	Please make it a little cheaper.
Clerk	Then……, give me just 26,000 won.
Nancy	How much is it all together?
Clerk	Um……, it's 33,000 won all together.
Nancy	Here is 40,000 won.
Clerk	Thank you.
	Here is the change, 7,000 won.

NOUN	얼마 how much; some amount
	천 1,000
	원 a 'won' (Korean currency)
	셔츠 shirts
	모두 all
	거스름돈 change (money)

VERB	비싸다 (be) expensive
	싸다 (be) cheap

ADVERB	너무 too much, very much, excessively
	좀 a little: some

PARTICLE	______만 a particle meaning 'only'; just

ADDITIONAL VOCABULARY	잔돈 small change: loose money
	십 / 백 / 천 / 만 10 / 100 / 1,000 / 10,000

Expressions

"얼마입니까?"   (How much is it?) in Formal Polite

"얼마예요?"   (How much is it?) in Informal Polite

"음......."   (Um.......)

1) _____게 is adverbial verb suffix that modifiesthe following verb.

2) _____(아, 어, 여) 주다 is used to express 'to do something as a favour'.

3) Noun이에요 / Noun예요 is the Informal Polite form of the identification verb이다.

    a) N이에요 is used when the noun ends in a consonant:
    이 분은 선생님이에요. (This person is a teacher.)

    b) N예요 is used after a vowel:
    저는 제임스예요. (I'm James.)

Exercise 13

Translate the following sentences in Formal Polite.

1) How much is it?

2) It's 850 won.

3) It's too expensive.

4) No, it's not expensive.

5) It's 87,000 won all together.

6) Do you have the change?

7) How much is that shirt?

8) Here is the shirt.

9) Then, pay just 35,000 won.

10) I don't have small change.

Situation: Michael and Jenny go to a Korean restaurant. This is dialogue among
Michael, Jenny, and a waiter.

Dialogue

웨이터   어서 오세요!

　　　　몇 분이십니까?

마이클   두 사람입니다.

웨이터   이리 오십시오.

　　　　여기 앉으십시오.

마이클과 제니   감사합니다.

웨이터   여기 메뉴가 있습니다.

마이클   고맙습니다.

웨이터   무엇을 드시겠습니까?

제니   저는 비빔밥을 먹겠습니다.

마이클   육개장은 아주 맵습니까?

웨이터   아니요, 그렇게 맵지 않습니다.

마이클   그럼, 육개장을 주십시오.

웨이터   예, 알겠습니다.

Waiter	Welcome!
	How many people are you?
Michael	We are two.
Waiter	Please come this way.
	Sit down here please.
Michael & Jenny	Thank you.
Waiter	Here is a menu.
Michael	Thanks.
Waiter	What are you going to have?
Jenny	I'm going to eat bibimbap.
Michael	Is yukgaejang very hot?
Waiter	No, it's not so hot.
Michael	Then, give me a yukgaejang.
Waiter	Yes, I understand.

Vocabulary

NOUN	비빔밥 'bibimbap' (boiled rice with assorted vegetables)
	육개장 'yukgaejang' (hot shredded beef soup and rice)

VERB	앉다 to sit down
	드시다 an honorific verb of 'to eat (먹다)'
	주다 to give
	맵다 (be) spicy hot ('ㅂ' irregular verb)

ADVERB	이리 this way
	그렇게 that much

ADDITIONAL VOCABULARY)	저리 in that way
	그리 in the way
	짜다 (be) salty

Expressions

"알겠습니다."   "I see." "I understand."

Grammar Notes

1) _____이십니까?   honorific form of '입니다'

2) 'ㅂ' irregular verbs: 맵다

   The stem 'ㅂ' becomes '오' or '우' before a vowel:

   맵 + 어요 〉 매 + 우 + 어요 〉 매워요
   춥 + 어요 〉 추 + 우 + 어요 〉 추워요

   * 춥다 (be) cold

Translate the following sentences in Informal Polite.

1) Please come this way. (Honorific)

2) What are you going to eat? (Honorific)

3) Here is a menu.

4) Are you going to eat bibimbap? (honorific)

5) It's not that salty.

6) Then, give me a bibimbap. (honorific)

7) Yes, I understand.

8) Please, sit down here. (Honorific)

9) Are you going to eat it? (honorific)

10) Here is a yukgaejang.

Situation: Thomas is inviting Linda to his birthday party.

Dialogue

토마스 린다, 오늘 저녁에 시간이 있으면 우리 집에 와요.

린다 왜요? 무슨 일이 있어요?

토마스 오늘이 제 생일이에요.

생일 파티에 친구들을 초대했어요.

린다 아, 그래요?

생일을 축하해요!

토마스 감사합니다.

린다 몇 시에 모두 모여요?

토마스 7시에 모이지만, 일찍 와도 좋아요.

린다 그럼, 6시 반에 가겠어요.

Translation

Thomas	Linda, please come to my house if you have time this evening.
Linda	Why? What's up?
Thomas	Today is my birthday.
	I invited friends to birthday party.
Linda	Oh, is that right?
	Happy birthday!
Thomas	Thank you!
Linda	What time do you all gather?
Thomas	We meet at 7 o'clock, but it's okay even if you come early.
Linda	Then, I'll go at 6:30.

Vocabulary

NOUN	
	저녁 evening
	우리 1) we 2) our
	집 a house; a home
	모두 all; everybody; everything
	일 a happening; a work; a matter
	제 1) I (제가) 2) my (저의 〉 제)
	생일 a birthday
	친구 a friend
	반 half (30 minutes)
	들 plural suffix

NOUN MODIFIER	무슨 what kind of; some kind of

VERB	
	초대하다 to invite
	축하하다 to congratulate
	모이다 to gather

ADVERB	
	왜 why
	일찍 early

Expressions

"왜요?"   "Why is it so?" (Informal Polite)

Grammar Notes

1) _____(으)면   if, when

비가 오지 않으면 가겠습니다
(If it doesn't rain, I'll go.)

2) Noun(_____V)예요. / Noun(_____C)이에요.

제니는 제 친구예요. / 저는 학생이에요.
(Jenny is my friend.)   (I'm a student.)

3) _____지만   although, however

비가 오지만, 저는 학교에 가겠습니다
(Although it's raining, I'll go to school.)

4) _____(아, 어, 여)도 좋다   it's okay to do…

지금 가도 좋습니다.
(It's okay if you go now.)

5) _____겠어요 Informal Polite of _____겠습니다.

Exercise 15

Translate the following sentences in Formal Polite.

1) What's up?

2) Congratulations!

3) You can go now.

4) Are you going to invite your friends?

5) If you have a time, please come the party (파티).

6) Jenny goes at 2 o'clock, but Linda goes at 3 o'clock.

7) Then, will you come to my home this evening?

8) Are they all gathering today?

9) Is today Jenny's birthday?

10) Although it's 4 o'clock now, I'm going home today early.

Situation: Thomas is calling to talk to his friend Joan, and Joan's father picks up the phone.

Dialogue

토마스　여보세요?

(조앤의) 아버지　여보세요?

토마스　저는 조앤의 학교 친구 토마스입니다.

아버지　아, 그래요?

　　　　나는 조앤의 아버지예요.

토마스　아, 안녕하세요?

　　　　지금 조앤이 있습니까?

아버지　아니요, 조앤은 지금 집에 없어요.

　　　　아침에 상점에 일하러 가서 아직 돌아오지 않았어요.

토마스　아, 그렇습니까?

　　　　조앤이 보통 몇 시쯤 집에 돌아옵니까?

아버지　6시쯤 돌아와요.

　　　　7시쯤 다시 전화해봐요.

토마스　네, 그러겠습니다.

　　　　그럼, 안녕히 계세요.

Thomas	Hello?
(Joan's) Father	Hello?
Thomas	I'm Thomas, one of Joan's friends at school.
Father	Oh, is that right? I'm Joan's father.
Thomas	Oh, how are you? Is Joan home?
Father	No, she is not at home now.
	She went to a store to work this morning and has not returned home yet.
Thomas	Oh, is that right?
	What time does she usually return home?
Father	She returns home around 6 o'clock.
	Please try to call around7 o'clock again.
Thomas	Yes, I will do that.
	Then, good-bye!

Vocabulary

NOUN	아버지 a father
	아침 morning; a breakfast
	상점 a store

VERB	돌아오다 to return
	그러다 to do so; contraction of '그렇게 하다'
	전화하다 to phone

ADVERB	아직	yet
	보통	usually
	다시	again

| SUFFIX | 쯤 | about; around |

ADDITIONAL VOCABULARY	벌써	already
	가게	a store; a shop
	점심	lunch; lunch time
	저녁	dinner; evening

Expressions

"실례지만, 누구십니까?"　　"Excuse, who is calling?"

"누구를 찾으십니까?"　　"Whom do you want to talk to?"

"잘못 걸었습니다."　　"You've dialed a wrong number."

* 잘못 (adverb) mistakenly　　걸다 to dial

1) _____(으)러 가다 / 오다   go or come to do something

나는 일하러 갑니다.   I'm going to work.
나는 공부하러 왔습니다.   I came to study.

2) _____(아, 어, 여) 보다

(a) do it to find out (how it is)
(b) have an experience
그 사람을 만나 보았습니다.   met a person...
그것을 먹어 보았습니다.   ate it...
그것을 공부해 보았습니다.   studied it ...

3) 쯤 is a suffix meaning 'about' 'approximately,' and attached after a noun:

몇 시쯤   about what time
네 시간쯤   about 4 hours

Translate the following sentences into Korean in the speech form indicated in the bracket:

(1) Formal Polite	(2) Informal Polite	(4) Informal Plain

1) May I talk to Jane? (1)

2) You've dialed a wrong number. (1)

3) Is Mr. Lee (이) there? (Honorific) (2)

4) I'll try to go to the university tomorrow. (2)

5) Around how many people came to the party? (4)

6) Jane went to China to meet her friend. (2)

7) Would you try to go there to meet the person? (2)

8) Will you go to the restaurant to eat lunch together? (1)

9) Let's go to downtown to see the movie tomorrow. (4)

10) The person didn't come back home yet. (4)

Situation: Jennifer is introducing herself in front of others.

Introduction

안녕하세요?

제 이름은 제니퍼입니다.

저는 영국에서 왔어요.

런던대학교에서 문학과 심리학을 공부했어요.

저는 작년에 한국에 교환학생으로 왔어요.

현재, 저는 하나대학교에서 한국어를 공부하고 있습니다.

한국어는 어렵지만, 저는 열심히 공부하고 있습니다.

날마다, 다섯 시간 한국말을 공부합니다.

저는 월요일부터 금요일까지 공부해요.

주중에는 공부하고, 주말에는 친구들과 재미있게 지냅니다.

내년에는 한국역사를 공부하려고 합니다.

만나서 반갑습니다.

감사합니다.

Hello.

My name is Jennifer.

I came from England.

I studied literature and psychology at the University of London.

I came to Korea last year as an exchange student.

Presently, I'm studying the Korean language at Hana University.

Although the Korean language is difficult, I'm studying hard.

Everyday, I study Korean for five hours.

I study from Monday to Friday.

I study during the weekdays, and have a good time with my friends on the weekend.

I'm going to study Korean history next year.

I'm glad to meet you.

Thank you!

Vocabulary

NOUN	
문학	literature
심리학	psychology
교환 학생	an exchange student
월요일	Monday
금요일	Friday
주중	weekdays
주말	weekend
내년	next year

VERB	
어렵다	(be) difficult 'ㅂ' irregular verb
재미있다	(be) interesting '재미있게' is adverbial form of 재미있다

ADVERB	
열심히	hard; diligently

PARTICLE	
Noun (으)로	(1) toward (2) by means of (3) as; status

ADDITIONAL VOCABULARY	
월요일	Monday
화요일	Tuesday
수요일	Wednesday
목요일	Thursday
금요일	Fridayday
토요일	Saturday
일요일	Sunday
조금 / 좀	a little

Grammar Notes

1) Noun(으)로 (a) consonant '으로': 식당으로   (b) vowel '로': 학교로

   (1) toward: head for

   저는 시내로 갑니다. (I'm heading for downtown.)

   (2) by: by means of

   버스로 왔습니다. (I came by a bus.)

   (3) as: status

   선생님으로 일합니다. (I'm working as a teacher.)

2) _____고 있다 / 있었다   Present / Past Progressive

   This structure is used to explain when an action is in progress:

   지금 비가 오고 있습니다. (It is raining right now.)
   제니는 공부하고 있었습니다. (Jenny was studying.)

3) _____고

   This connective verb ending is used to connect more than one action or state. It means 'and':

   그 사람을 만나고 학교에 갔습니다.
   (I met the person and went to school.)

4) _____게 'verb stem + 게' makes an adverbial form of a verb:

   맵다: 맵 + 게 하다 (to make it spicy hot)
   어렵다: 어렵 + 게 하다 (to make it difficult)
   재미있다: 재미있 + 게 하다 (to make it a fun)

5) _____(으)려고 하다   intend to:

   그 사람을 만나려고 합니다. (I'm going to meet the person.)

Translate the following sentences into Korean in Informal Polite.

1) I'm working here as a teacher.

2) It's fun. However, it's a little difficult.

3) Next year, Thomas is going to Paris (파리) to meet Susan.

4) I came from Japan to study Korean literature.

5) Presently, I'm working for a bank.

6) Jennifer went to the States by a bus.

7) Thomas studied psychology in England and came to Canada.

8) I went ate lunch and met the person.

9) Because it rained yesterday, I didn't go there.

10) It was very interesting, so I studied hard.

Situation: Thomas is writing a letter to his mother from Korea.

Letter

사랑하는 어머니께,
저는 어제 아침에 한국에 도착했습니다.
어제 오자 마자 학교에 갔습니다.
미국에서 같이 공부한 제인을 거기에서 만났습니다.

저는 제인과 같이 한국 식당에 가서 저녁을 먹었습니다.
저는 불고기를 먹고 제인은 갈비를 먹었습니다.
음식이 모두 정말 맛있었습니다.
그리고 시장에 가서 필요한 물건을 좀 샀습니다.
물건 값은 그렇게 비싸지 않았습니다.

오늘은 비가 옵니다.
어머니는 지금 무엇을 하십니까?
저는 항상 어머니를 생각합니다.
편지 자주 쓰겠습니다.
어머니, 사랑해요.
안녕히 계세요.

2016년 5월 10일
서울에서
토마스 올림

To my beloved mother,

I arrived in Korea yesterday morning.

I went to school as soon as I arrived yesterday.

I met Jane there, with whom I studied together in the States.

I went to a Korean restaurant with Jane and had a dinner.

I ate bulgogi and Jane ate galbi.

The foods were all really delicious.

After that, I went to a market and bought some necessary things.

The price of things was not that expensive.

It's raining today.

What are you doing now, mom?

I always think of you.

I'll write to you often.

Mom, I love you!

Bye.

May 10, 2016

From Seoul

Thomas

Vocabulary

NOUN	불고기 bulgogi
	갈비 galbi
	음식 food
	맛 taste
	시장 1) a market 2) mayor
	물건 a thing; an object
	값 price
	비 rain
	편지 a letter
	올림 a humble form of 'from' (addressor)
VERB	도착하다 to arrive
	필요하다 (be) necessary
	사다 to buy
	비싸다 (be) expensive
	생각하다 to think
	쓰다 to write
ADVERB	모두 all
	정말 really
	자주 often
CONJUNCTION	그리고 and; then

<table>
<tr><td>ADDITIONAL
VOCABULARY</td><td>싸다   (be) cheap; inexpensive
눈   1) snow   2) eye</td></tr>
</table>

<table>
<tr><td>PARTICLE</td><td>께 honorific word for 에게 (to a person or other animated creatures)
a) 존에게 To John
b) 교수님께 To Professor</td></tr>
</table>

Grammar Notes

(1) _____자 마자   as soon as:

토마스가 가자 마자, 제니가 왔습니다
(As soon as Thomas left, Jenny came.)

2) AV. stem (ㄴ / 은) + Noun

A modifying structure of an action verb (AV) that has been completed. It is used to describe the following noun:

(a) _____ㄴ is attached to a vowel ending
한국말을 공부하 + ㄴ 사람 〉 한국말을 공부한 사람
(a person who studied Korean)

(b) _____은 is attached to consonant ending:
점심을 먹 + 은 사람 〉 점심을 먹은 사람
(a person who ate lunch)

Translate the following sentences into Korean in the speech form indicated in the bracket.

(1) Formal Polite	(2) Informal Polite	(4) Informal Plain

1) I phoned him as soon as I arrived in Korea. (4)

2) The person I met in the market yesterday is Jane. (1)

3) I intend to meet the friend tomorrow and go to the store together. (1)

4) I was studying literature, and Jennifer was studying psychology. (2)

5) I went to the hospital yesterday and met Mr. Kim. (4)

6) The house was not so good. (4)

7) I often think of the person I met in England. (2)

8) Please buy the cap if it's not expensive. (1)

9) I met the student whom I studied together with in China. (2)

10) I will often write a letter to a friend in Korea. (1)

Write a letter to a friend in Korean.

Sending an email (1)

Situation: John is sending an email to a friend on his birthday. The speech form of Lesson 19 is Informal Plain (Appendix 1: Table 4), Lesson 20 is Formal Plain (Appendix 1: Table 3).

Text

수진에게!

오늘은 11월 10일, 내 생일이야.

아침 일찍 일어났어.

날씨가 참 좋았어.

나는 학교 체육관에 가서 한 시간 동안 운동을 했어.

오늘은 오후에 수업들이 있었어.

경제학과 철학이야.

나는 경제학을 전공하지만, 철학도 좋아해.

철학은 좀 어렵지만, 다음 학기에도 계속하려고 해.

저녁에는 친구들이 기숙사에서 내 생일 파티를 해 주었어.

생일 케이크를 자르고 맥주도 마셨어.

친구들이 많이 와서 아주 재미있게 놀았어.

내일은 시험이 있어.

그러나 준비를 많이 했으니까, 나는 걱정하지 않아.

안녕.

존

To Soojin.

Today is November 10, it's my birthday.

I woke up very early.

The weather was really nice.

I went to the school gym and exercised for one hour.

I had classes in the afternoon.

They are economics and philosophy.

I major in economics, however I like philosophy as well.

Although philosophy is a little difficult, I'm going to continue studying it next term as well.

My friends had a birthday party for me in the evening at the school residence.

We cut cake and also drank beers.

Many friends came and we had a very good time.

I have an exam tomorrow.

However, since I've prepared a lot for it, I don't worry.

Bye.

John

NOUN	
내	I or my
생일	a birthday
오전	morning (a.m.)
날씨	weather
체육관	gym
동안	an interval; a while
운동	(physical) exercises; sports
오후	afternoon (p.m.)
수업(들)	a class; (school) lessons
경제학	economics
철학	philosophy
다음	next
기숙사	a dormitory
파티	party
케이크	cake
시험	a test; an exam

VERB	
일어나다	to wake up; to get up
전공하다	to major
어렵다	(be) difficult (ㅂ irregular verb)
계속하다	to continue
자르다	to slice
마시다	to drink
놀다	to play; not to do anything ('ㄹ' irregular verb)
준비(하다)	to prepare
걱정하다	to worry

<table>
<tr><td>ADVERB</td><td>일찍   early
참   really
많이   a lot</td></tr>
</table>

<table>
<tr><td>CONJUNCTION</td><td>그러나   but; however</td></tr>
</table>

Expressions

"파티를 했어요."   "We had a party.'"

"안녕."   "Bye." in Plain Speech Form

Grammar Notes

야 / 이야   Informal Plain of '이다'

'야' is attached after a vowel ending: 그 사람은 제니야. (The person is Jenny.)
'이야' is attached after a consonant ending: 제니는 학생이야. (Jenny is a student.)

Change the dialogues of Lesson 19 into Formal Polite.

1) 오늘은 11월 10일, 내 생일이야.

2) 아침 일찍 일어났어.

3) 날씨가 참 좋았어.

4) 학교 체육관에 가서 한 시간 동안 운동을 했어.

5) 오늘은 오후에 수업들이 있었어.

6) 경제학과 철학이야.

7) 나는 경제학을 전공하지만 철학도 좋아해.

8) 철학은 좀 어렵지만 다음 학기에도 계속하려고 해.

9) 저녁에는 친구들이 기숙사에서 내 생일 파티를 해 주었어.

10) 생일 케이크도 자르고 맥주도 마셨어.

11) 친구들이 많이 와서 아주 재미있게 놀았어.

12) 내일은 시험이 있어.

13) 그러나 준비를 많이 했으니까 걱정하지 않아.

14) 안녕.

15) 존

Situation: John is sending an email to a friend on his birthday. The speech form of Lesson 19 is Informal Plain (Appendix 1: Table 4), Lesson 20 is Formal Plain (Appendix 1: Table 3).

Text

수진에게

오늘은 11월 10일, 내 생일이다.

아침 일찍 일어났다.

날씨가 참 좋았다.

나는 학교 체육관에 가서 한 시간 동안 운동을 했다.

오늘은 오후에 수업들이 있었다.

경제학과 철학이다.

나는 경제학을 전공하지만, 철학도 좋아한다.

철학은 좀 어렵지만, 다음 학기에도 계속하려고 한다.

저녁에는 친구들이 기숙사에서 내 생일 파티를 해 주었다.

생일 케이크를 자르고 맥주도 마셨다.

친구들이 많이 와서 아주 재미있게 놀았다.

내일은 시험이 있다.

그러나 준비를 많이 했으니까, 나는 걱정하지 않는다.

안녕.

존

To Soojin,

Today is November 10, it's my birthday.

I woke up very early.

The weather was really nice.

I went to the school gym and exercised for one hour.

I had classes in the afternoon.

They are economics and philosophy.

I major in economics, however I like philosophy as well.

Although philosophy is a little difficult, I'm going to continue studying it next

term as well.

My friends had a birthday party for me in the evening at the school residence.

We cut cake and also drank beers.

Many friends came and we had a very good time.

I have an exam tomorrow.

However, since I've prepared a lot for it, I don't worry.

Bye.

John

1) _____다 / _____이다 Formal Plain of '이다'. (Appendix 1: Table 6)

_____다 is attached after vowel ending:

그 사람은 제니다. (The person is Jenny.)

_____이다 is attached after consonant ending:

제니는 학생이다. (Jenny is a student.)

2) 있었다 is Formal Plain of the past tense of 있다. (Appendix 1: Table 7)

Exercise 20

Write an email to a friend in either Informal Plain or Formal Plain.

Sending an email (3)

Situation: John is sending an email to a person about the reason he could not keep an appointment with him.

Text

선생님께,

오늘 약속을 못 지켜서 죄송합니다.

아침을 먹고 갑자기 배가 아팠습니다.

약국에 가서 약을 사서 먹었으나 조금도 낫지 않았습니다.

그래서 가까운 병원에 가서 의사 선생님을 만났습니다.

의사 선생님은 처방전을 주셨습니다.

저는 그 약을 먹고 집에서 몇 시간 잤습니다.

저녁에는 많이 좋아졌습니다.

내일은 괜찮을 것 같습니다.

내일 오전에 선생님 사무실에 가겠습니다.

오늘, 정말 죄송합니다.

내일 뵙겠습니다.

존 올림

Sir,

I'm sorry that I couldn't keep my appointment today.

After I had breakfast, I suddenly had an upset stomach.

I went to a pharmacy to buy medicine and I ate it; however, I didn't feel any better.

Therefore I went to a hospital and met a doctor.

The doctor gave me a prescription.

I had the medicine and slept a few hours at home.

I felt much better in the evening.

It seems that tomorrow will be okay.

I'll come to your office tomorrow morning.

I'm really sorry for today.

I'll see you tomorrow.

From John

Vocabulary

NOUN	약속 appointment 배 1) stomach 2) pear 3) boat 약국 a drugstore 처방전 a prescription 의사 (선생님) a doctor

VERB	지키다 to keep; to preserve 죄송하다 (be) sorry 사다 to buy 먹다 to eat 아프다 (be) sick ('으' irregular verb) 낫다 1) (be) cured 2) (be) better ('ㅅ' irregular verb) 주다 to give 자다 to sleep 좋아지다 to become better; to get better 괜찮다 (be) okay 가깝다 (be) near; closed ('ㅂ' irregular verb)

ADVERB	못 can not 갑자기 all of sudden 조금도 even a little bit 정말 really

CONJUNCTION	그래서 then; therefore 그리고 and

Grammar Notes

1) _____(았, 었, 였)으나: it was (or did) but...

학교에 갔으나 그 사람을 만나지 않았습니다.
(I went to school, but I didn't meet the person.)

2) SV_____(으)ㄴ 것 같다: it seems to

그 물건이 좋은 것 같습니다.
(The item seems to be good.)

3) SV_____(으)ㄹ 것 같다: it will be... (guess / assume)

그것이 좋을 것 같아요.
(I think it will be good.)

4) verb stem + 시 (honorific stem) + 었습니다 (past tense ending)

주 + 시 + 었습니다 〉 주셨습니다

Write a diary for one day.

APPENDICES

TABLE 1: Formal Polite Style

1.1 Verb Ending of a Sentence

Declarative (Statement)	____(C)습니다. ____(V)ㅂ니다.
Interrogative (Question)	____(C)습니까? ____(V)ㅂ니까?
Imperative (Command)	____(C)으십시오. ____(V)십시오.
Propositive (Proposal)	____(C)읍시다. ____(V)ㅂ시다.

* '_' represents the stem of a verb

1.2 Present : Past & Positive : Negative Statement

	Positive	Negative
Present	____(V)ㅂ니다. ____(C)습니다.	____지 않습니다. OR (안 + statement)
Past	____았습니다. ____었습니다. ____였습니다. (하였 > 했)	____지 않았습니다. OR (안 + statement)

TABLE 2: Informal Polite Style

2.1   Verb Ending of a Sentence

Declarative (Statement)	_____아요. _____어요. _____여요. (하여 〉 해)
Interrogative (Question)	_____아요? _____어요? _____여요? (하여 〉 해)
Imperative (Command)	_____아요. _____어요. _____여요. (하여 〉 해)
Propositive (Proposal)	_____아요. _____어요. _____여요. (하여 〉 해)

* '–' represents the stem of a verb

2.2   Present : Past & Positive : Negative Statement

	Positive	Negative
Present	_____아요. _____어요. _____여요. (하여 〉 해)	_____지 않아요. OR (안 + statement)
Past	_____았어요. _____었어요. _____였어요. (하였 〉 했)	_____지 않았어요. OR (안 + statement)

ACTION VERB

3.1 Verb Ending of a Sentence

Declarative (Statement)	_____(V)ㄴ다. _____(C)는다.
Interrogative (Question)	_____니? _____느냐? / _____는가?
Imperative (Command)	_____(아, 어, 여)라. 하여 〉 해 _____거라.
Propositive (Proposal)	_____자.

* '–' represents the stem of a verb

3.2 Present : Past & Positive : Negative Statement

	Positive	Negative
Present	_____(V)ㄴ다. _____(C)는다.	_____지 않는다. OR (안 + statement)
Past	_____았다. _____었다. _____였다 (하였 〉 했)	_____지 않았다. OR (안 + statement)

TABLE 4: Informal Plain Style

4.1 Verb Ending of a Sentence

Declarative (Statement)	_____아. _____어. _____여. (하여 〉 해)
Interrogative (Question)	_____아? _____어? _____여? (하여 〉 해)
Imperative (Command)	_____아. _____어. _____여. (하여 〉 해)
Propositive (Proposal)	_____아. _____어. _____여. (하여 〉 해)

* '–' represents the stem of a verb

4.2 Present : Past & Positive : Negative Statement

	Positive	Negative
Present	_____아. _____어. _____여. (하여 〉 해)	_____지 않아. OR (안 + statement)
Past	_____았어. _____었어. _____였어. (하였 〉 했)	_____지 않았어. OR (안 + statement)

TABLE 5: Formal Plain Style (State Verbs)

5.1 Verb Ending of a Sentence

Declarative (Statement)	(Basic Form)
Interrogative (Question)	_____(으)니? _____(으)냐? _____ㄴ가? / 은가?
Imperative (Command)	N / A
Propositive (Proposal)	N / A

* '_' represents the stem of a verb

5.2 Present : Past & Positive : Negative Statement

	Positive	Negative
Present	Basic Form	_____지 않다. OR (안 + statement)
Past	_____았다. _____었다. _____였다. (하였 > 했)	_____지 않았다. OR (안 + statement)

1) Honorific Expressions

There are a few ways to show respect to the subject of a sentence. Generally, the honorific stem '(으)시' is attached to the original verb stem. This forms a new verb stem, then this new stem is conjugated with various verb endings. '시' is attached after a vowel ending, and '으시' is attached after a consonant ending:

가 + 시　〉　가시　　　　　가시 + ㅂ니다　〉　가십니다
잡 + 으시　〉　잡으시　　　잡으시 + ㅂ니다　〉　잡으십니다

However, some verbs have completely separate honorific verbs. In this case, this honorific verbs must be used instead of adding '(으)시' to the original verb. Only a limited number of Korean verbs have separate honorific verbs. There are also honorific nouns and particles. Please refer to the following for a list of some verbs, nouns and particles.

(a) Honorific Verbs:

to eat	먹다 〉 잡수시다 / 드시다
to sleep	자다 〉 주무시다
to die	죽다 〉 돌아가시다
to exist	있다 〉 계시다 / 안녕하시다
to talk	말하다 〉 말씀하시다

(b) Honorific Nouns:

person	사람 〉 분
meal	밥 〉 진지
talk	말 〉 말씀
residence	집 〉 댁
age	나이 〉 연세
illness	병 〉 병환

(c) Honorific Particles

| Subject marker | 이 / 가 〉 께서 |
| Dative marker | 에게 〉 께 |

2) Humble Expressions

There is another way of showing respect to the subject. This is called 'Humble Expressions.' In contrast to Honorific Expressions, when using Humble Expressions the speaker employs the 'humble form of a verb.' This humble form of a verb 'humbly' describes one's own actions to show respect:

to take or bring a person along	데리고 오다 / 가다 〉 모시고 오다 / 가다
to give	주다 〉 드리다
to talk	말하다 / 이야기하다 〉 말씀드리다
to see / meet	보다 〉 뵙다

There are different types of irregular verbs in Korean.

a) '으' Irregular verbs: The vowel of the last syllable is deleted before a vowel.
'ㅡ' is omitted before a vowel and replaced with either ㅏ or ㅓ
depending on the vowel of the preceding syllable.

    (a) If the vowel is 'ㅏ' or 'ㅗ', the omitted 'ㅡ' becomes 'ㅏ':
       바쁘다 〉 바빠 + 았습니다 〉 바빴습니다

    (b) If the vowel is 'ㅓ' 'ㅜ' or 'ㅡ', it becomes 'ㅓ':
       예쁘다 (be pretty): 예쁩니다 (present) ⟶ 예뻤습니다 (past)
       e.g., 크다 (be big)   쓰다(to use / to write / be bitter)   나쁘다(be bad)

b) 'ㄷ' Irregular verbs: The stem final ㄷ becomes ㄹ before a vowel.

걷다 (to walk): 걷습니다 (present) ⟶ 걸었습니다 (past)
e.g., 듣다 (to hear), 싣다 (to load), 묻다 (to ask a question)

Regular verbs: 닫다 (to close), 믿다 (to trust), 받다 (to receive)

c) 'ㅅ' Irregular verbs: The stem final ㅅ is deleted before a vowel.

짓다 (to build): 짓습니다 (present) ⟶ 지었습니다 (past)
e.g., 긋다 (to draw), 잇다 (to connect), 낫다 (better, to get well)

Regular verbs: 벗다 (to take off), 씻다 (to wash), 웃다 (to laugh)

d) 'ㅂ' Irregular verbs: The stem final ㅂ becomes 오 or 우 before a vowel.

춥다 (be cold): 춥습니다 (present) ⟶ 추웠습니다 (past)
e.g., 덥다 (be hot), 어렵다 (be difficult), 돕다 (to help)

Regular verb: 잡다 (to catch)

e) 'ㄹ' Irregular verbs: The stem final ㄹ is deleted before ㄴ, ㅂ, ㅅ, 오, 으

놀다 (to play)   ⟶   놉니다 (present)

e.g., 알다 (to know), 팔다 (to sell), 불다 (to blow)

f) '르' Irregular verbs: The vowel 으 is deleted before a vowel and ㄹ is doubled.

모르다 (not to know): 모릅니다 (present)   ⟶   몰랐습니다 (past)

e.g., 부르다 (to sing, call), 흐르다 (to flow), 다르다 (be different)

g) 'ㅎ' Irregular verbs: The stem final ㅎ is deleted before ㄴ, ㅁ, 으.

파랗다 (be blue)   ⟶   파란 (a modifier: 파란 + 집)

e.g., 노랗다 (be yellow) 빨갛다 (be red)

Regular verb: 좋다 (be good)

좋다 (good)   ⟶   좋은 (a modifier: 좋은 + 사람)

Exercise 0:2

1. 가구　2. 노란　3. 도장　4. 시골　5. 반찬
6. 이름　7. 전차　8. 아침　9. 저녁　10. 병원
11. 골목　12. 라면　13. 만두　14. 안경　15. 파전
16. 향기　17. 달력　18. 신문　19. 감자　20. 풍속

Exercise 1

1) 처음 뵙겠습니다.
2) 반갑습니다.
3) 제 이름은 존입니다.
4) 마이클은 캐나다 사람입니까?
5) 네. 그렇습니다.
6) 조앤은 일본 사람이 아닙니다.
7) 아, 조앤은 일본 사람이 아닙니까?
8) 제 이름은 제니가 아닙니다.
9) 그렇습니까?
10) 안녕히 계십시오.

Exercise 2

1) 저 학생은 누구입니까?
2) 그 분은 이 학교의 선생님입니까?
3) 토마스는 제니의 친구입니다.
4) 그 집은 제 친구의 집입니다.
5) 티나는 제니의 친구입니까?
6) 아니요. 티나는 제니의 친구가 아닙니다.
7) 그 분은 그 대학교의 교수님이 아닙니다.
8) 베티는 이 대학원의 학생입니까?
9) 박 선생님은 저 학교의 선생님입니까?
10) 아니요. 박 선생님은 저 학교의 선생님이 아닙니다.

Exercise 3

1) 저 건물은 무엇입니까?
2) 그것은 대학교입니다.
3) 저는 시청에서 일합니다.
4) 저것도 병원입니까?
5) 그것은 병원이 아닙니다.
6) 저것은 백화점이 아닙니까?
7) 그 건물은 제니의 학교입니까?
8) 저는 그 건물에서 일합니다.
9) 그 백화점은 참 좋습니까?
10) 제니도 시청에서 일합니까?

Exercise 4

1) 지금 어디에 가십니까?
2) 저는 학교에 갑니다.
3) 대학교에서 무엇을 공부합니까?
4) 저는 한국말을 공부합니다.
5) 한국 역사도 공부합니까?
6) 아니요, 저는 지금 한국 역사를 공부하지 않습니다.

7) 어디에서 영어를 공부합니까?

8) 저는 오늘 시내에 가지 않습니다.

9) 내일 무엇을 하십니까?

10) 그럼, 내일 학교에서 같이 공부합시다.

Exercise 5

1) 영국에서 그 사람을 만나지 않았습니까?

2) 작년에 어느 분을 만나셨습니까?

3) 어느 나라에서 오셨습니까?

4) 누가 수잔을 사랑했습니까?

5) 수잔은 누구를 사랑했습니까?

6) 오늘 학교에서 그 사람을 만나지 않습니까?

7) 마이클과 제니는 학교에 처음 왔습니다.

8) 제니는 중국에서 오지 않았습니다.

9) 저는 병원에 가서 그 분을 만났습니다.

10) 언제 한국에서 캐나다에 왔습니까?

Exercise 6:1

1) 03 : 35　　(　세　)시　(　삼십오　)분
2) 07 : 28　　(　일곱　)시　(　이십팔　)분
3) 08 : 46　　(　여덟　)시　(　사십육　)분
4) 12 : 12　　(　열두　)시　(　십이　)분
5) 11 : 05　　(　열한　)시　(　오　)분
6) 05 : 20　　(　다섯　)시　(　이십　)분
7) 01 : 17　　(　한　)시　(　십칠　)분
8) 09 : 31　　(　아홉　)시　(　삼십일　)분
9) 04 : 59　　(　네　)시　(　오십구　)분
10) 06 : 11　　(　여섯　)시　(　십일　)분

Exercise 6:2

1) 내일 시간이 있습니까?

2) 저는 내일 아주 바쁩니다.

3) 언제 영화를 보러 갔습니까?

4) 저는 오늘 시간이 없습니다.

5) 그 분을 만나러 시청에 가겠습니까?

6) 내일 저의(제) 집에서 만납시다.

7) 저는 어제 저녁에 시간이 없었습니다.

8) 오늘 다섯 시 전에 학교에서 만납시다.

9) 그럼, 한 시간 후에 만나겠습니까?

10) 네, 학교에서 같이 공부합시다.

Exercise 7

1) 지금 어디에 있습니까?

2) 저는 코리아호텔에 있습니다.

3) 그 호텔은 백화점 뒤에 있습니까?

4) 그 대학교는 이 근처에 있습니다.

5) 아홉 시에 집에 있었습니까?

6) 저는 어제 저녁에 집에 없었습니다.

7) 내일 여기에 또 오십시오.

8) 그 건물은 그 호텔 오른쪽에 있습니다.

9) 거기에 같이 갑시다.

10) 대단히(매우) 감사합니다!

Exercise 8

1) 그 사람은 언제 와요?

2) 어디에서 한국말을 공부했어요?

3) 지금 저는 학교에 있어요.

4) 내일 시장에 가요.

5) 지금 은행에 가요.

6) 언제 한국에 오셨어요?

7) 지금 아주 바빠요?

8) 지금 바쁘지 않아요.

9) 오늘 시간이 있어요?

10) 그럼, 같이 가요.

Exercise 9

Exercise 9

1) 어느 운동을 특히 좋아해요?

2) 지금 무슨 일을 하세요?

3) 이 시장은 참 좋아요.

4) 어제 날씨는 좋지 않았어요.

5) 모든 운동을 좋아하세요?

6) 오늘 학교에 가지 않아요?

7) 존은 은행에서 일하지 않았어요.

8) 저는 그 일을 별로 좋아하지 않았어요.

9) 저는 그 사람을 매우 좋아했어요.

10) 모든 학교가 좋아요.

Exercise 10

테리: 아이고, 벌써 1시가 되었습니다.

조앤, 점심 먹었습니까?

조앤: 아니요, 아직 안 먹었습니다.

테리: 저는 아주 배고픕니다!

조앤: 저도 그렇습니다.

같이 밥 먹으러 갑시다.

테리: 어느 식당에 가겠습니까?

국수집에 가겠습니까? 불고기집에 가겠습니까?

조앤: 무척 배고프니까, 불고기집에 갑시다.

테리: 좋아요, 빨리 갑시다.

Exercise 11

1) 한국말을 공부하러 한국에 가요.

2) 그 사람은 바쁘니까 내일 그 사람을 만나.

3) 저는 제 친구를 만나러 거기에 빨리 갔습니다.

4) 박 선생님을 같이 만날까요?

5) 저는 학교에서 무척 배고팠습니다.

6) 어느 학교에서 공부했어요?

7) 국수를 먹을까? 불고기를 먹을까?

8) 무슨 운동을 좋아했습니까?

9) 저는 특히 그 백화점을 좋아했어요.

10) 그 은행은 그 식당 뒤에 있어.

Exercise 12

1) 운동 모자를 찾습니까?

2) 파란 모자는 어떻습니까?

3) 운동 모자는 어디에 있습니까?

4) 초록 신발은 없습니다.

5) 누구를 찾습니까?

6) 그 분은 저기에 있습니다.

7) 그 파란 건물은 병원입니다.

8) 파란 모자가 있습니까?

9) 아니요, 저는 파란 모자가 없습니다.

10) 여러 가지 신발이 있습니다.

1) 얼마입니까?

2) 팔백오십 원입니다.

3) 너무 비쌉니다.

4) 아니요. 비싸지 않습니다.

5) 모두 팔천칠백 원입니다.

6) 거스름돈이 있습니까?

7) 저 셔츠는 얼마입니까?

8) 여기 셔츠가 있습니다.

9) 그럼, 삼만 오천 원만 주십시오.

10) 거스름돈이 없습니다.

1) 이리 오세요.

2) 무엇을 드시겠어요?

3) 여기 메뉴가 있어요.

4) 비빔밥을 드시겠어요?

5) 짜지 않아요.

6) 그럼, 비빔밥을 주세요.

7) 네, 알겠어요.

8) 여기 앉으세요.

9) 그것을 드세요?

10) 육개장이 있어요.

1) 무슨 일이 있습니까?

2) 축하합니다!

3) 지금 가도 좋습니다.

4) 친구들을 초대하겠습니까?

5) 시간이 있으면, 파티에 오십시오.

6) 제니는 두 시에 가지만, 린다는 세 시에 갑니다.

7) 그럼, 오늘 저녁에 저의 집에 오겠습니까?

8) 오늘 그들 모두 모입니까?

9) 오늘은 제니의 생일입니까?

10) 지금은 네 시지만, 저는 오늘 일찍 집에 갑니다.

1) 제인과 말할 수(통화할 수) 있습니까?

2) 잘못 걸었습니다

3) 이 선생님이 거기에 계세요?

4) 저는 내일 대학교에 가겠어요.

5) 그 파티에 몇 사람 쯤 왔어?

6) 제인은 친구를 만나러 중국에 갔어요.

7) 그 사람을 만나러 거기에 가겠어요?

8) 점심을 같이 먹으러 그 식당에 가겠습니까?

9) 내일 영화를 보러 시내에 가.

10) 그 사람은 아직 집에 오지 않았어.

1) 저는 선생님으로 여기에서 일해요.

2) 재미있어요. 하지만, 조금 어려워요.

3) 내년에, 토마스는 수잔을 만나러 파리에 가요.

4) 저는 한국 문학을 공부하려고 일본에서 왔어요.

5) 현재, 저는 은행에서 일해요.

6) 제니퍼는 버스로 미국에 갔어요.

7) 토마스는 영국에서 심리학을 공부하고 캐나다에 왔어요.

8) 저는 점심을 먹고 그 사람을 만났어요.

9) 어제는 비가 왔기 때문에, 저는 거기에 가지 않았어요.

10) 매우 재미있어서 저는 열심히 공부했어요.

Exercise 18.1

1) 나는 한국에 도착하자마자 그 사람에게 전화했어.

2) 어제 제가 시장에서 만난 사람은 제인입니다.

3) 저는 내일 친구를 만나서 같이 상점에 가겠습니다.

4) 저는 문학을 공부하고 있었고, 제니퍼는 심리학을 공부하고 있었어요.

5) 나는 어제 병원에 가서 김 선생님을 만났어.

6) 그 집은 아주 좋지 않았어.

7) 저는 가끔 영국에서 만난 그 사람을 생각해요.

8) 비싸지 않으면 그 모자를 사십시오.

9) 저는 중국에서 함께 공부한 학생을 만났어요.

10) 저는 한국에 있는 친구에게 자주 편지를 쓰겠습니다.

Exercise 19

1) 오늘은 11월 10일, 제 생일입니다.

2) 아침 일찍 일어났습니다.

3) 날씨가 참 좋았습니다.

4) 학교 체육관에 가서 한 시간 동안 운동을 했습니다.

5) 오늘은 오후에 수업들이 있었습니다.

6) 경제학과 철입니다.

7) 저는 경제학을 전공하지만 철학도 좋아합니다.

8) 철학은 좀 어렵지만 다음 학기에도 계속하려고 합니다.

9) 저녁에는 친구들이 기숙사에서 제 생일 파티를 해 주었습니다.

10) 생일 케이크도 자르고 맥주도 마셨습니다.

11) 친구들이 많이 와서 아주 재미있게 놀았습니다.

12) 내일은 시험이 있습니다.

13) 그러나 준비를 많이 했으니까 걱정하지 않습니다.

14) 안녕히 계십시오.

15) 존 올림

Exercise 18.2

Example

사랑하는 크리스틴에게,

나는 어제 아침에 캐나다에 도착했어.
어제 오자 마자 학교에 가서 한국어 교수님을 만났어.
교수님과 나는 한국에 대하여 이야기를 했어.
그리고 교수님과 나는 같이 한국 식당에 가서 점심을 먹었어.
나는 감자탕을 먹고 교수님은 된장찌개를 드셨어.
한국 음식을 먹으니까 한국 생각이 났어.
서녁에 시내에 기서 한국 영화를 봤어.

그래서 어제는 밤 늦게 집에 돌아왔어.

나는 지금 커피를 마시고 있어.
지금 무엇을 하고 있어?
나는 가끔 너를 생각해.
편지 자주 쓸게.
잘 지내.

2016년 11월 10일
워털루에서
토니

Example

제니스에게,

요즘 어떻게 지내?
나는 잘 지내고 있어.
오늘은 날씨가 좀 추웠지만, 나는 아침 운동을
1시간 30분 쯤 했어.
그리고 학교에 가서 수업을 했어.
나는 경제학을 전공하지만, 한국 문화를 좋아해.
그래서 다음 학기에도 한국 문화 공부를 계속하려고 해.

저녁에는 집에서 동생 토니의 생일 파티를 했어.
생일 케이크를 자르고 불고기도 먹었어.
토니는 매우 즐거워했어.

내일은 경제학 시험이 있어.
경제학은 어렵기 때문에 준비를 많이 했어.
오늘 밤에도 시험 공부를 계속 하려고 해.
다음에 또 메일 보낼게.
안녕.

2016년 11월 11일
워털루에서
테리

Example

11월 25일 눈

오늘은 무척 바빴다.
아침에 학교에 가서 네 시간 공부를 했다.
마이클을 만나 도서관 앞의 케페테리아에 가서 점
심을 먹었다.
마이클은 피자를 먹고, 나는 햄버거를 먹었다.

그 후 우리는 시내에 가서 모자를 사고 한국 영화
도 봤다.
한국 식당에 가서 감자탕과 순두부를 먹었다.
마이클과 나는 한국 음식을 참 좋아한다.
마이클과 나는 한국의 음식에 대해서 이야기를
했다.

10시 쯤 집에 돌아왔다.
조금 전부터 열이 조금 나고 기침도 났다.
애드빌을 먹었지만, 좋아지지 않는다.
내일은 의사 선생님을 만나러 병원에 가야겠다.
의사가 처방해 준 약을 먹으면 괜찮아지기 때문
이다.
내일도 아침부터 수업이 있으니까 일찍 자야겠다.